# ADVANCING
# CONFIDENTLY

*by Peter Bachmann*

PUBLISHER: TwoSixty Productions
© Peter Bachmann, 2016
978-0-9837364-2-4
Cover Photo: Tim Bradley
Book Design: Jana Winters Parkin
Formatting: Janel Baird
Editors: DeNae Handy, Claire Kinder

# ADVANCING CONFIDENTLY

*If one* **advances confidently**

*in the direction of his dreams*

*and endeavors to live the life he has imagined,*

*he will meet with a success unexpected*

*in common hours.*

—Henry David Thoreau, *Walden*

# TABLE OF CONTENTS

*To the memory of Scott Studenmund*

*A free soul*

Charlie — check out
p. 227

Best,
Peter Bochimor

# INTRODUCTION

At 6:00 a.m., June 10, 2014, I received the phone call I had feared and dreaded. Scott Studenmund, Flintridge Prep graduate of 2008, Green Beret, United States Army Special Forces, had been killed on a mission in Afghanistan. He was twenty-four.

I had known Scott since he was twelve, when he entered seventh grade in our school. During his six years with us he was fiercely individual, crafting his high school experience around his tastes and interests, unintimidated by faculty, family, or peer pressure. Whatever the focus—American History, history of warfare, football, track—he pursued it wholeheartedly and with abandon. When he graduated, he headed for college and college football, but he knew where his heart lay, and after a semester he left to join the military. For the next five years, he pushed himself to excel in the most demanding and dangerous assignments. Whether learning Arabic, marksmanship, or diving, he willed himself to the top of the unparalleled competition. By the time he was deployed to Afghanistan in early 2014, he was the person he had consciously sculpted himself to be: physically, intellectually, and spiritually. His mother Jaynie told me: "I take comfort in knowing that he was doing what he loved."

Scott loved his country and fought on its behalf with "the last full measure of devotion." But he also loved and respected himself, enough to design a life that suited his unique vision, by, in Thoreau's words, "confidently advancing in the direction of his dreams." In order to do so, he had to withstand well-meaning second guessing from multiple people in his life, who wondered why he left college, why he didn't hold out for an Academy appointment, which his National Merit recognition might have warranted, why he should enter the military and harm's way at all, with so many safer, more lucrative options before him. Through it all, he refused to settle for anyone's dreams but his own. He lived and died insisting on the freedom to fashion a life according to his own sense of self.

In 1955, Senator John F. Kennedy's *Profiles in Courage* studied eight senators throughout history who risked their political futures on an issue of principle. Most of us are neither soldiers nor senators, but, like Scott and those rare politicians, each of us has the option—and maybe the obligation—to seek our own best selves. Yet the temptation for young people today to settle for something less is pervasive. There is a crisis of confidence among many students and parents, anxious about getting into the "best" college, selecting a "practical" major, finding a "sensible" job in a "safe" career.

"I'd really like to go to the number fifteen college, but I got into number twelve," explained one student to me recently, presumably allowing the *US News & World Report* ranking to make her decision for her.

"I don't really like my business major, but it's practical," explained another at a dinner last month.

"My job's boring, but it pays well and it's steady."

These quotes come from good people with talent, who have the freedom and opportunity to "advance confidently in the direction of their dreams," but settle for less, without knowing if settling is necessary. There is a desperation to their tone, but as Thoreau reminds us, "it is a characteristic of wisdom not to do desperate things." Fear and anxiety threaten to trump imagination and responsible risk-taking that can lead to more rewarding and sometimes more lucrative outcomes.

The consequences of this trend are not only personal but national. In a recent panel of contemporary authors, David McCullough, Walter Isaacson, and Buzz Aldrin agreed that the nation was becoming, in Aldrin's words, "risk-averse," and have all written books reminding us of a more confident heritage. Isaacson's recent *The Innovators* traces the creative link between art and science in the technological revolution. His previous books include biographies of innovators Benjamin Franklin, Albert Einstein and Steve Jobs. McCullough's recent book, *The Wright Brothers,* comes on the heels of studies about the building of the Brooklyn Bridge and the Panama Canal. Buzz Aldrin has walked on the moon. None of these authors, or their subjects, are risk-averse.

I'm not advocating a particular choice of life, since Scott Studenmund and Thoreau chose very different paths, but authentic choice itself. This book celebrates confident dreamers who have advanced and achieved by making the most of their freedom in orchestrating their lives.

The people profiled in the following pages have another common denominator: they are products of a liberal arts education, which Robert Hutchins calls "the arts of freedom." While in school these people studied broadly across the arts and sciences, pursued a passion, and found that route ultimately, paradoxically, the most practical one of all. These examples give hope to people that confidence, courage, conviction, passion and imagination can pay off professionally and personally. The quotes in the appendix suggest that yearning countless young people have to be passionate and free.

Part one of this book traces some of the influences on my friends and me that have propelled our dreams. Part two, the heart of this book, chronicles individuals who have successfully imagined and realized highly individual lives appropriate to them. The epilogue circles back to the boldest liberal artist of them all, while the appendix quotes 250 high school seniors who dream of advancing confidently.

My oldest teacher quoted in the book was born in 1899, my youngest student in 1997. These two dreamers—and all those born between—would have understood one another's sensibility perfectly.

# CHAPTER ONE:
*The Labyrinth of Berkeley,*
*September 2013*

In 2005 Daniel Pink published *A Whole New Mind:*
*Why Right-Brainers Will Rule the Future*, arguing that the
"information age," which has favored sequential, logical,
analytical thinking, is evolving into the "conceptual age,"
which will be led by creators and empathizers, who stress
the non-linear, intuitive and holistic right hemisphere of the
brain. He reasons that, as retrieving information digitally
becomes a pervasive skill, creativity will be the key competitive advantage. Provocatively, he asserts that the MFA
(Master of Fine Arts) will become the new MBA (Master of
Business Administration).

What methods, he asks, will we employ to stimulate the increasingly crucial right hemisphere of the brain? A century ago, novelist Marcel Proust famously described an adult character's bite into a "petite madeleine," a cake from childhood that unlocks his involuntary memory of his past in order to understand his life. So what are our 21st Century petite madeleines?

Pink thinks one of them is the labyrinth, currently popular in churches, hospitals, gardens, and sometimes homes and offices. He states:

> *"The labyrinth is a spiraling walking course. When you enter your goal is to find a path to the center, stop, turn around, and walk back out. Labyrinths are a form of moving meditation; labyrinths can be centering....labyrinths free the right brain."*

People in search of right hemisphere insight and inspiration may walk another's labyrinth such as the one in San Francisco's Grace Cathedral or the Johns Hopkins Medical Center, or they can design their own. Without knowing it at the time, I recently created my own labyrinth, my own

moving meditation, in the form of a spiraling walk in Berkeley, indirectly leading me to the campus center, and back out
again. In the process I tapped into ancient memories, and a
new understanding of how my past influences my present.

## WALK #1: THE OUTER CIRCLE

Emerging from Café Milano on Bancroft Way on a Friday
afternoon, I smiled as I recalled the laughter at the table with
my former students as they traded yarns of triumphs and
tribulations at Berkeley. It was a relaxed moment, which I
enjoyed largely as an observer from another generation.

My most direct route to my destination was up the
street. Sometimes, however, the most obvious practical path
is not ultimately the most rewarding. So I walked down the
block, creating a more circuitous path by familiar settings
of my youth. I recalled that labyrinth can be symbolic of
pilgrimage, and I was on a pilgrimage into my past. Lauren
Artress has stated: "When people walk into the labyrinth
they begin to see their whole life."

I was looking for eighteen to twenty, my first two years
I spent in this neighborhood, buying books in the store on
my left, to go to class on campus to my right. But my true

classroom, I realized as I circled left and back up Durant Avenue, was the student housing I gazed at near the corner of Telegraph. The third floor of Spens-Black Hall had been the center of my universe for those two years: dorm room, classroom, common room, home to hundreds of hours of days with intellectual exchange and nights with all the ecstasy and agony of that moment in life. Continuing up the block, I smelled coffee from Kip's, where we went when we missed breakfast, and brats from Top Dog, where we finished off evenings. Completing my cycle, I entered the Hotel Durant, where I would soon reunite with friends from those days, more than forty years later, to celebrate the Residential Program in History and Literature, the intellectual and personal springboard into our futures.

The Program was born in 1968, due to the efforts of Professor William Slottman, who believed that even the largest universities should provide an education to each student one at a time, in cloistered surroundings, where the distinction between school and personal life could evaporate, promoting an engagement with ideas as part of daily reality. Students would live together, eat together, read, write and talk together in close proximity with their teachers, combining the best qualities of a small school and world-class research center.

A number of us who had been part of the Program during the years 1968-1972 had agreed on a reunion at the campus Faculty Club the next day, but tonight I would be joining a smaller group of classmates. As freshmen we had been inseparable, mostly out of fondness, but also from circumstance, since we often travelled as a group from lunch (few made it to breakfast) to afternoon seminars, ending in somebody's room until the late hours.

Walking into the Durant Bar, I saw familiar faces: Mark and Jane Kriss, who had met in The Program, married, raised two boys, and embarked on a series of entrepreneurial ventures; Judi Kalitzki, her passion for language and literature fired at eighteen, now a writing professor at Washington; Joan Wright, philosophy major, attorney, horsewoman, opera lover. All independent spirits, briefly reunited in nostalgic community.

Throughout the night, memory of our times together emerged and re-sorted itself with every tale from the past. Stories came tumbling as each person re-kindled some version of our eighteen-year-old selves. Certain accounts were classics widely recognized, others new, sometimes adding an additional clue to the reality of our youth, reminding us of both the reliability and fallibility of memory. As each person updated the table on more recent events, I was struck, in every case, by the strong sense of self, the devotion to personal vision and passion. New homes had been created in different parts of the country, new families and careers, but I heard common threads running over the decades, through each life. Hair was shorter, sometimes grayer, but as Judi noted, "voices don't change," and those voices, like an ancient familiar song, transported me back into a world I rarely accessed. I was back in room 307, our dorm room with ten people spread over beds and chairs, standing in the doorway competing in storytelling, the room erupting in laughter. It hadn't all been fun, but tonight my petite madeleine was warm sentiment. I'd found the friendships of the past. What part of myself would the next day uncover?

## WALK #2: THE MIDDLE RING

Following breakfast, I began walking, another circuitous route by signposts of my past. This time it would be onto campus, through the plazas, back down Telegraph Avenue, and up around Channing. I took an umbrella, since it was misty, the clouds and fog adding to the feeling of otherworldliness. As I passed the upper campus softball field, I remembered our season-ending triumph over Priestly Hall, fueled by a late inning hit by Verlyn Klinkenborg, who presently was teaching one of my former students at Yale. As I saw a familiar bench, I remembered sitting there with Bruce Kirmmse, one of my sophomore teachers, for over thirty minutes one November afternoon. He asked me about my personal background, and told me his own. He had been a graduate student at Berkeley for years, partly because he had re-written his dissertation on Danish philosopher Sorgen Kierkegaard from scratch, apparently in search of perfection. His tale of uncompromising standards both inspired and concerned me. Would he ever get it done? Would he find a permanent gig? I needn't have worried. He became a world-renowned Kierkegaard scholar, recognized by the Queen of Denmark. His quiet but fierce self-confidence, coupled with his kind interest in me, flooded back as I strolled slowly by.

Passing through Sather Gate, I came to the outdoor tables of Sproul Plaza, where one day I bumped into Stephen Greenblatt and Richard Freudenheim, my two freshman English teachers. I recalled that we lingered there at length, two teachers, one student, talking about Shakespeare conversation in our sections, reviewing both the plays and the class personalities. Stephen complimented me on my increased participation in discussion, specifically my recent comment on the Falstaff/Hal relationship in *Henry IV.*

Stephen Greenblatt, soon-to-be international wunderkind, remembered my comments? I talked even more in class after that day.

Sauntering off campus, I wandered down Telegraph Avenue, suspecting that the white-haired pony-tailed vendor had been a brown-haired pony-tailed vendor four decades earlier. As I walked by the corner of Durant, I remembered bumping into Bill Nestrick, a sophomore English teacher, who knitted his diverse passions for film, the Renaissance, opera, and nineteenth century novels, into a unique multimedia teaching career. We chatted about class, and he suggested coffee.

Bill Nestrick wants to have coffee with me?

Turning back up Channing toward residential Unit One, the final home of The Program, I came upon Slottman Hall, and stopped. Beyond directing The Program, Bill Slottman was a legendary teacher in the University. His Hapsburg course, in Dwinelle's multi-hundred seat room, drew standing room only each year. He reminded one of Jack Benny, in

his buttoned gray suit, hand in one pocket, so straight-faced
and bone dry that the witticisms struck like thunderclaps.
Many took his course for the humor, but soon discovered an
erudition and intellectual integrity that commanded respect.
He embodied the teaching idealism that, as he once said,
"makes education a calling and not just an employment." I
spent my freshman year in close quarters with him, at one
point in a section of four students. He directed me in two
major research papers, quietly guiding me in the direction
of certain sources and perspectives, always encouraging me,
filling me with intellectual self-confidence. His lengthy, kindly written comments on my work alternated generous praise
with gentle suggestion: "You may wish to vary your historical diet…but not too much." More than anyone that first
year, Slottman gave me the self-assurance and courage to
make my own way. So I lingered a bit beside his hall, before
returning to The Durant and our reunion lunch.


**WALK #3: THE INNER RING**

As we gathered in the hotel lobby, Judi announced:
"I know it's the long way around, but we need to walk
through Sather Gate, by Wheeler Hall, and across the Creek
to get to the Faculty Club."

Another circuitous walk. So we followed her path by Wheeler, home of the English Department and some of our favorite professors. We came to Sather Tower, the Gothic Revival Campanile at the iconic center of campus. The clock and bell tower, patterned after St. Mark's Square in Venice, can be seen from miles away, symbol of the continuing tradition of learning. As we crossed Strawberry Creek, we entered the glade framed by redwoods, and faced the 1902 Craftsman style retreat, quiet respite for a century of teachers.

Inside we met several other classmates, and a number of Program alumni a year or two older. Mingling and lunch were pleasant, if slightly awkward, as we tried to position ourselves among less familiar faces. Eventually one of the reunion coordinators offered a suggestion:

"Why don't we go around the room, and each of us can say something about The Program and its impact on us."

My immediate reaction: oh God, pass the wine. The potential for self-indulgence, redundancy, and narcissism seemed limitless. Would we hear about every offspring's tortuous slog through high school? Each person's self-congratulatory or victimization-laden career tale? Or worse, public proclamations of physical or emotional infirmities? I girded my loins.

What followed, however, was the most soulful of hours, as we were transported into our past by heartfelt expressions of gratitude to the Program, for providing a safe haven during the tumultuous times, lifelong friendships, space to develop dreams and discover enduring passions for the curriculum that knew no conventional boundaries and encouraged imaginative connections across disciplines. Paradoxically, the theoretical and symbolic had become practically useful, and intimate communalism had produced independent spirits of unique individuality.

"I discovered my passion for language and literature and the resolve to become an English professor."

"My marketing and branding business constantly requires me to think across conventional limits."

"The Program was a home at a time when I needed one."

All spoke of the warmth and vibrancy of the faculty, and for a while I marinated in the nostalgic glow of Edenic memories of this caring, intellectual and personal cocoon.

Then somebody said:

"The Program was a great place to grapple with the reality of the tumult of the Berkeley campus, and the sixties: People's Park, Cambodia, Laos."

Laos. Suddenly I was jolted back to a day in winter 1971, when our forces invaded Laos as part of the Vietnam strategy. Berkeley made the front page national news that week as a center of student protest, and many of us in The Program were full participants, regarding it in part as serious business, part street theatre. I remembered the sunny afternoon as thousands of us moved through the streets toward Sproul Plaza, on campus, The Stones' "Street Fighting Man" blaring from speakers up and down the blocks. We freshmen were furious, determined, principled, and also pretty pumped that the revolution was finally coming to us. In the Plaza, speaker after speaker castigated the invasion, until one finally suggested that we take our protest down to Berkeley City Hall. For the next hour we migrated through city streets until we reached our destination, and found it—closed. When we looked inside, we saw Alameda County Sheriffs' Deputies, with billy clubs, tear gas, and guns. Not the relatively amiable campus police, who diplomatically contained paying customers, but future Attorney General Ed Meese's troops, armed for battle.

I never knew what erupted to turn the confrontation into chaos, but soon the streets were strewn with deputies chasing protesters, filling the air with tear gas and making arrests. When I observed one officer chasing a young girl with his club extended, I saw red. At that moment the violent impulse of the protest movement made sense to me, as I conjured up every image and ideology of the left, our policy embodying in my mind the savagery of an imperial power. I had never had such a moment of moral certainty in my life.

Eventually, I made my way back toward campus, and came to Durant Avenue by the dorm, stumbling on a sight I had forgotten about on my sentimental walk yesterday. There was an Atomic Energy Commission Car, flipped on its hood and ablaze, with protesters clapping and cheering.

Sitting in the Faculty Club luxuriating in the reunion, I was hammered by my memory of the moral complexity that struck me in the street that day. As I watched the savagery of the left compete with the savagery of the right, I was forced out of the simple, comforting melodramatic world

into the tragic world of complexity. Neither police nor protesters were either angel or devil. Rather we were locked
in a tragic unfolding of national crisis. And I was forced to
remember, on the reunion day in Faculty Glade, that there
had been nothing simple about being eighteen.

The night after the protest, I left the contemporary world
of strife to do my homework. I needed to get ready for
Greenblatt and *Hamlet*, so I opened to this passage in Act V,
as the Prince holds up the skull of his former court jester:

> *"Alas, poor Yorick! I knew him, Horatio: a fellow*
> *of infinite jest, of most excellent fancy: he hath*
> *borne me on his back a thousand times; and now,*
> *how abhorred in my imagination it is!"*

Hamlet's nostalgic memory of the vibrant, living Yorick,
romantic in its illusory timelessness, is contrasted with the
brutal truth of the dead skull, that end point in time of the
history that awaits us all.

I put my book down. Twice in one day, once in the
street and once in Shakespeare, I had slammed into complexity, confronted with competing truths. In both cases, my
journey had been from the comforting certainty of one sim-

ple vision, either protester righteousness or Yorick's infinite jest, into a complex vision that needed to accommodate a burning car and Yorick's finite skull.

Two weeks later, we read Act IV of Shakespeare's *The Tempest*. It is a play set upon an island, overseen by a magician, Prospero, who conjures up a masque, a beautiful mythological entertainment for his daughter and future son-in-law. During the entertainment, the enchanted young man proclaims: "Let me live here forever."

The ultimate romantic, comic fantasy: let's stop time, suspend reality in a simple paradise. But as Prospero gently reminds him, we are not creatures of romance, but of history:

> *"We are such stuff*
>
> *As dreams are made on; and our little life*
>
> *Is rounded with a sleep."*

With all the romantic, almost illusory comforts of The Program cloister, the teachers constantly confronted us with complexity, challenging us when our answers were too pat. One time Greenblatt called a comment of mine "perverse," challenging my simplicity. When a classmate called the Roman Empire "fascist," Slottman cautioned him against easy categories. They knew they were preparing to send us from the cloister of the dorm to the crossroads of real life, and wanted the books and discussions to fortify us.

Sitting in the comforts of the reunion, I realized that the Program's final gift to us was a sense of complexity. The Program offered us intimacy, but insisted upon complexity, developed through reading, writing, talking, and personal engagement. As much as the friendships and faculty, we were celebrating that gift today.

At that point, I realized that my labyrinth walk was complete. I had found the center of my journey in the Faculty Glade. The three historic sites of the Program had been converted to other purposes, but its spiritual home lay in this spot where all our teachers who had practiced their craft as vocation could congregate at this center—and then, like any good labyrinth, would turn around and walk out. For the purpose of any labyrinth, like good teaching, is to guide you to the center, so you can walk back out into life renewed.

As we walked out of the reunion, several of us stood at the front of the Faculty Club, looking to the lawn, the redwoods, and the Campanile in the background. For a moment, time seemed suspended.

"It's the prettiest place on campus," my friend Mark said quietly. We all nodded, smiled, took it in for one final moment, then hugged and headed back into history in our cars and our individual lives and our individual histories.

# CHAPTER **TWO**:
*Teachers — Robert Hutchins and Stephen Greenblatt*

In 2005, the center of the Berkeley labyrinth was the Faculty Club. Our reunion prompted me to consider the qualities of my teachers that made them so effective. Beyond their superb scholarship, each was deeply collaborative, but passionately, fearlessly individual in style, tastes, and interests, as if their individuality and collaboration fueled one another.

All of these teachers were influential. Two teachers in my life, one from the Program, one from without, were transformational, by demonstrating educational values by which I live today. I have been a teacher since I was twenty-two, a school administrator since thirty, and have held the examples of these two men as the basis of my philosophy and practice. Because of them, I read the books that I read, do the work that I do, and hold the values that I hold.

The first, Robert Maynard Hutchins, taught me largely from afar, through writing and lectures, since I visited with him personally fewer than ten times in my life. Yet he articulately insisted that complete lives required three components: professional, public, and private fulfillment. One prepared for those lives through broad-based liberal education in the arts and sciences, understanding that learning is a lifelong enterprise. These principles resonate in everything I do.

When I first encountered Hutchins' essays in high school, his vision of education—argued consistently from age thirty to seventy-eight—seemed organic to his nature. From childhood he excelled in school, sailing through each level sensationally. A prodigy, his success as a student and professor at Yale Law School was such that he became the law school dean at age twenty-eight. By thirty he was President of the University of Chicago, heralded in the national press as America's most brilliant young educator.

So I was shocked to learn, upon reading Harry Ashmore's biography of Hutchins, *Unseasonable Truths*, that he came to Chicago with no coherent educational philosophy, and found a distinguished university that apparently lacked one as well. Ashmore recounts:

> *"Upon his precipitate elevation to the rank of university president, Robert Hutchins took stock of his own learning and recognized that he had arrived at the age of thirty "with some knowledge of the Bible, of Shakespeare, of Faust, of one dialogue of Plato, and of the opinions of many semi-literate and a few literate judges, and that was about all."*

In short, one of the most celebrated intellectuals in America came to regard himself as an intellectual fake. Of course he could succeed at Chicago through responsible administering, fundraising, and resource management—the normal purviews of university presidents. Yet, at the moment when the world was showering honors, comforts and opportunities upon him, the man who frequently warned against "unexamined assumptions" examined his own, and found them lacking. Nobody expected Hutchins to re-educate himself, or transform undergraduate education. In fact, an entrenched faculty preferred to be left alone.

The faulty assumptions that Hutchins discovered were that he himself was properly educated, and that his new university was delivering a proper education to its students. So during his first year as president, despite the exhausting demands of his new job, he embarked on a year's immersion in a classical education that included philosophers, literary artists, historians, scientists, and mathematicians.

In sculpting a serious liberal arts education for himself at the age of thirty, Hutchins harnessed philosophy in the service of the most practical purposes: how am I going to do my job? How am I going to run this university in the most effective way possible? To answer this question he turned to that most practical of philosophers: Aristotle.

Aristotle was a biologist. He valued understanding the nature of things, and believed all things—objects, people, organizations, culture—should realize the highest potential of their nature. As philosopher Michael Sandal notes, for Aristotle the purpose of a flute is to be played well. The purpose of an acorn is to become an oak. So Hutchins began to ask a question largely absent from education in 1930: What is the purpose of a university? The common answer was economic: to enable graduates to flourish in the workplace, and to provide workers with the general knowledge for prosperity. Hutchins agreed. He simply insisted that it was not the university's only purpose.

Following Aristotle's logic, Hutchins explored the nature of humans and society, and discovered multiple potentials in each. Humans could create prosperity, but they could also create justice. The great, rich society could also be the fair, just society. And prosperous individuals could also be happy, authentic, thoughtful and generous individuals.

Therefore, Hutchins concluded, in order for individuals and societies to reach their potential, education must fulfill multiple purposes. That was the *nature* of education if it was to realize its full potential.

In many of his mature writings, Hutchins emphasized three purposes of education, each complementing and leveraging the others: professional, public, and private. A fully-realized human being was one who thought critically and imaginatively as a result of a broadly-based education, who was prepared for the professional workplace, the public forum of participatory democracy, and a rewarding private life. And Hutchins warned, prosperity, democracy and personal happiness are all interdependent, with one unable to flourish indefinitely without the others.

So for Hutchins, the modern road leading to innovation, diversity, human rights and creativity, began with a Greek thinker from 2000 years ago offering wisdom for the future. As Homer illustrated even before Aristotle, the victories of the son utilize the sword of the father: lean back to spring forward.

In the decades to come, Hutchins would champion a liberal arts curriculum for undergraduates, cutting edge physics, and a new school of economics on the same campus. That Hutchins himself disagreed with many of the ideas presented by his world class faculty was precisely the point:

> *"Education is a kind of continuing dialogue,*
> *and a dialogue assumes different points of view."*

One prepared for a complex, diverse, dynamic world through argument and inquiry, privileging data and logic over personal preferences. And an essential part of education was to help people discover their authentic selves, not some pre-packaged facsimile.

By the fall of 1930, he felt prepared, with his colleague Mortimer Adler, to pilot a seminar in The Great Books for twenty freshmen. My father was in that class, and regarded it as the springboard for his later life. As a seminar leader, Hutchins was a great questioner—imaginative, ironic and demanding—but truly tough only on anyone coming unprepared. His written comments on papers could be pointed: "Should be cut by half. Which half doesn't matter."

The class promoted an intellectual fearlessness, akin to Hutchins' own willingness to reinvent himself at thirty. Satisfied that his pilot was a success, he pronounced Chicago's general curriculum as "unfit for free men" and created The Great Books as the cornerstone of the undergraduate experience. Turning his eye on what he regarded as the hypocrisy of college athletics, he abolished football ("why don't we just hire the Bears?"). Soon afterwards he began an adult Great Books class in downtown Chicago:

> *"What is proposed here is interminable liberal education....One cannot expect to store up an education in childhood that will last all of life. What one can do in youth is to acquire the discipline and habits that will make it possible for one to continue to educate oneself throughout life."*

Hutchins continued to reinvent himself throughout his life. After twenty-two controversial years at Chicago, he migrated to the Ford Foundation, where he promoted global education and world peace, until a nervous board pieced him off with his own foundation, the Fund for the Republic, in Pasadena. By 1959, he had moved to Santa Barbara—my hometown—to create The Center for the Study of Democratic Institutions, where he gathered thinkers known for vigorous conversation and controversy: Harry Ashmore, fresh from the Little Rock school crisis; anti-apartheid Bishop Edmund Crowther, recently exiled from South Africa; Linus Pauling, Nobel Prize winner for physics and peace, arrested in peace demonstrations. Their common denominator: fearless devotion to their principles and passions.

Growing up near The Center with a father who counted many of these people as friends, including his former teacher Hutchins, I came under their influence in high school. While Hutchins' measured, controlled style seemed a polar opposite to the musicians I idolized (would Keith Richards be invited to The Center?), his insistence that education meant the search for "unexamined assumptions" seemed astounding and revolutionary. From Hutchins I learned that education was not a part-time classroom affair, but the

gateway to everything: career, personal and political freedom, self-awareness, values, personal fulfillment. Education
was "The Great Conversation" of thinkers connecting past,
present and future, conducted day and night, throughout an
entire life. Hutchins inspired and encouraged me to apply
to The Berkeley Residential Program. He placed education
at the center of my life, where it remains today.

## MARVELOUS DISPOSSESSION

I met Stephen Greenblatt during my first week of the
Program in the small seminar room of our dorm. He was
only twenty-six at the time, but also funny, unassuming, and
obviously brilliant. I visited his office in the early weeks
and we traded biographical tales, his resume being slightly fuller than mine. I noticed a book on his shelf entitled
*Three English Satirists: Waugh, Orwell, and Huxley.* "I wrote
that as an undergraduate," he said, offhandedly. He referenced his interest in Sir Walter Raleigh, a historical figure
self-fashioned into a cultural icon. "I discovered Raleigh as
a Fulbright Scholar at Cambridge," Stephen explained, "and
followed him through my doctorate at Yale."

Let me get this straight: this guy published a book as an undergraduate, was a Fulbright Scholar, got his doctorate, is in his second year as a Berkeley professor, and hasn't seen his twenty-seventh birthday. Stephen has continued to amaze over the decades, first while at Berkeley for almost thirty years, and now as University Professor at Harvard. His ideas on new historicism have influenced critical analysis in multiple disciplines, and he is in demand as a lecturer from Moscow to Berlin. In the nineties he served as a consultant on the Oscar-winning *Shakespeare in Love*, and his 2004 book *Will in the World* rode the bestseller lists. More recently, in 2012, he won the Pulitzer Prize and National Book Award for *Swerve: How the World Became Modern*. He's so famous he even appears on the *Colbert Report*.

First and foremost, he is a courageous and original thinker who, like Hutchins, breaks conventional patterns of thinking, drawing from multiple disciplines and studying unconventional sources in pursuit of his vision. Jonathan Bate has called his approach "the most influential strand of criticism over the past twenty-five years." Whether one agrees with his ideas on new historicism or not, he forces us to look at literature, painting, history, and travel writing with greater richness and complexity, forces questions about the relationship between culture, power, imagination, and beauty. He earns prizes from admirers, and takes critical heat from skeptics. Through it all he advances our understanding of The Great Conversation. I'm thrilled for Stephen's success, but grateful for more private reasons. In February 1971, in that cramped dorm living room, he gave me my North Star, my metaphor, and a priority for life. On that day, as we read Act V of Shakespeare's *The Tempest*, when the protagonist Prospero prepares to divest himself of supernatural power, just as Shakespeare prepared to retire from the stage, Stephen asked: "What would it mean to drown Shakespeare's books?"

The question first baffled, then terrified us. After burrowing into the concept and the question at length, the answer exploded among us:

> *"If we could drown the books we would no longer need them. Not because we had rejected them, but because we had absorbed them. We wouldn't need to own them, because we had internalized their meaning. All that perspective, poetry, shrewdness, insight. All that freedom. Possessing the books was a means to understanding them. The end game was a life that made Shakespeare's virtues your own."*

Director Peter Brook said:

*"With Shakespeare, one has something very extraordinary: a man who was not only 100% alive, but perhaps 1,000, 10,000…a million percent alive, this person walking through the streets of London (Shakespeare) must have lived each single moment with an incredible richness of awareness."*

So Shakespeare's phenomenal awareness would be my North Star, that perspective that allows one to be actor and audience at once, acting soulfully in your own life while maintaining the distance to craft it and interpret it. A magic brew of experience and understanding, knowing when to forget yourself in ecstasy, and when to pull back and re-member your reality, as Prospero had done in Act IV, when he was swept away in joyous celebration of his daughter's betrothal, but remembers (just in time) that people are com-ing to kill him.

So, with all of that awareness, who needs possessions? Well…I did. Even in the thrill of discovery, I couldn't kid myself. Much as I loved many of Thoreau's words, I could never land in his cabin in the woods. I liked heat, restaurants, and indoor plumbing too much, and a wallet full enough to take me on the travels I imagined. But neither Shakespeare nor Greenblatt invited me to forsake the material—certainly not best-selling Shakespeare, the prosperous real estate mogul of Stratford.

Near the end of *The Tempest* Prospero's daughter Miranda, who has seen only three men in her life on her island retreat, looks upon ten of them, and proclaims:

> *"Oh, wonder!*
>
> *How many goodly creatures are there here!*
>
> *How beauteous mankind is!*
>
> *O brave new world,*
>
> *That has such people in't! "*

Her father responds:

> *"Tis new to thee."*

Miranda's uncomplicated tribute is both touching and troubling, since she is looking upon half angels and half devils. *The Tempest* has been a warning against naïveté, as it describes a world in which pure innocence can be exploited. So Miranda is half wrong. But she's also half right, and far more admirable (admired Miranda) than her opposite, her cynical uncle Antonio, who views a non-white native for the first time, and pronounces him "no doubt marketable."

Shakespeare's foreshadowing of African slavery in a "brave new world?"

One of Stephen Greenblatt's themes, as a discussion leader and an author, was retaining our sense of wonder in a world where everyone and everything may be perceived by some as "marketable." In *The Tempest,* Shakespeare cunningly juxtaposes Miranda's delightful but dangerous innocence with her uncle's automatic urge to possess and sell "the other" from a foreign land. In his 1991 book, *Marvelous Possessions*, Greenblatt traces these contrasting impulses through the Age of Discovery, beginning with Christopher Columbus' report on his discovery of the new world:

> *"I found very many islands filled with people innumerable, and of them all I have taken possession."*

No doubt marketable?

He contrasts this chronicle with that of *The Travels of Sir John Mandeville* from the fourteenth century:

*"There are many different peoples in the new lands,*
*but who knows whom God loves?"*

Mandeville's wonder and Columbus' market are famously contrasted on the final page of F. Scott Fitzgerald's *The*
*Great Gatsby.*

> *"Gradually I became aware of the old island here that*
> *flowered once for Dutch sailor eyes, a fresh green*
> *breast of the new world. Its vanished trees, the trees*
> *that had made way for Gatsby's house, had once*
> *pandered in whispers to the last and greatest of all*
> *human dreams, for a transitory enchanted moment*
> *man must have held his breath in the presence of this*
> *continent, compelled into an aesthetic contemplation*
> *he neither understood nor desired, face to face for the*
> *last time in history with something commensurate*
> *with his capacity for wonder."*

The green breast is overtaken by the vulgar marketeers
Tom & Daisy, "careless people—they smashed up things
and creatures and then retreated back into their money or
vast carelessness . . . "

Fitzgerald offers no reconciliation beyond "boats against the current" and narrator Nick's return to the West. Shakespeare may suggest something more hopeful: perspective.

"Tis new to thee."

Prospero qualifies his daughter's wonder without destroying, fully conscious that brutal marketeers are there to be watched and checkmated. Realism that is not corrupted into cynicism; understanding the world as it is, yet committed to improving it.

On that day in the Program living room, I placed possessions in perspective, where I hope they have stayed. "Shakespeare's books inside me" would be my metaphor and Shakespeare's awareness my priority and ultimate North Star. So at that moment, Stephen gave me what he would later call a "marvelous dispossession," a cautionary perspective on the urge to acquire, exploit, and stratify. And he clarified and symbolized for me my urge for understanding, which built on Hutchins' vision, and sent me confidently in the direction of my dreams.

# CHAPTER THREE:
*Model – Bach Bachmann*

Teachers left me invaluable lessons, which are constantly present in my memory and their writings. Throughout
the decades, however, I felt I needed human reinforcement,
constantly reminding me to advance confidently, from
someone who knew my strong spots and my soft ones. I
needed a model, someone who embodied Thoreau's theme:
a courageous, sometimes brash, dreamer, who combined
his idealism with a canny realism. Fortunately, I found one
early in life, and kept him close for fifty years. I still live
with his legacy.

———————————————

At the end of my freshman year at Berkeley, I invited several friends to have dinner with my parents. They were happy to oblige, anticipating free food and drinks, polite conversation, and a fairly quick turnaround so they could hit the dorm parties.

They didn't realize that they were dealing with Bach Bachmann.

For the next four hours, spirits flowed, delectable platters of fusion food followed one another, while discussion topics moved from politics to sports, novels to business, all peppered by my father's stories, including this one:

It seemed a peddler with a donkey needed to cross the river, and found himself besieged with well-wishers on his left, encouraging him to move up river, while friends on the right urged him to cross further down. Not wishing to offend, he split the difference—he crossed in the middle, where a torrent swept away the donkey, who was drowned.

"Which just goes to show," my father explained, "that if you try to please everyone, you're going to lose your ass."

Later that night, my friend Terence said: "You didn't tell me about your father."

How do you prepare someone for an original?

The donkey story, which drew plenty of laughs, was told partly for my benefit. My father appreciated my amiability, but worried that I might be too anxious to please, too needy for approval, to strike out very far from the mainstream. One couldn't say the same about him.

He was born in Southside Chicago to an upstanding German Lutheran family, his heavily accented grandfather a warm presence in the home of his childhood. His dentist father, housemaker mother, and dietitian sister were all cut from the same traditional cloth. My father cut his own cloth from the outset, voracious for multiple experiences. By the time he entered the University of Chicago at seventeen, he had pursued American history, built a sailboat, played the violin, hit a double in Wrigley Field, defended (or tried to defend) against John Wooden on the basketball court, acted in school productions, and discovered French cuisine. Nobody else in his family followed any of these pursuits.

His life had begun robustly before college, but he always felt it achieved theme and purpose during his freshman year, in the Great Books seminar with Hutchins and Adler. There he discovered that ideas and life impacted one another, that books could be practical as well as theoretical counselors, that disagreement, conflict, and complexity were creative experiences necessary for growth, and that assumptions accepted by most people as fundamental truths should be examined carefully.

For example, "Why shouldn't I jump on a boat for the Caribbean?" he asked in his mid-twenties after his first successful real estate sale. So he did, and there met his future father-in-law, who introduced him to my mother. She was the light of his life for fifty-five years, but he would never have met her if he had followed conventional wisdom.

"Why shouldn't I join the army before I'm drafted?" Most friends were staying with their careers as long as possible, but his early entry led to officer candidate school, and eventually to a staff position with Patton in the Third Army in Europe, a defining experience in his life, both for executive experience and, far more profoundly, for his keen appreciation of war's tragedy, when he marched into Dachau Concentration Camp in 1945.

"Why shouldn't we move to California?" Friends and family thought my parents were crazy, giving up a successful business and familiar surroundings for an unknown future. Yet they went anyway, struggled for several years, and eventually caught the California Dream in its economic and culturally expansive years, settling in Santa Barbara, which witnessed the growth of a state university, the arrival of Hutchins and his center, engineering companies, and an unparalleled real estate boom.

"Why shouldn't we start our own business?" He and a partner cut loose from secure positions in another company, creating Pitts & Bachmann, defying most common business practices at the time. As soon as they could, they refrained from working as a salesman to avoid competing with employees. They introduced newcomers to a "romance tour" of Santa Barbara, focused on history, culture, and aesthetics, never once mentioning or viewing property until the magic of the town was properly appreciated. Advertising was never allowed to use the word "house." They were helping families find homes.

Everyone thought my father was wasteful, publishing *Lincoln's Thanksgiving Proclamation* each November and excerpts from *A Christmas Carol* each holiday season. He was, of course, indirectly and implicitly building a brand. And besides, he thought people should read Lincoln and

Dickens. A decade ago, they were proven right when the firm was sold to Sotheby's International.

So my father advanced confidently through middle age, secure in his ability to follow his own lights and strong in his conviction that others should do the same.

———————————————

Beginning in childhood, I noticed my father was different from my friends' parents. He was often at the center of any room, making people laugh with stories I often didn't understand, sometimes using me as an embarrassed straight man to set up the punch line. If I remarked that I found my Christmas Club interest rate low, he would have me speak to the banker, as I did at age eight. When I disagreed with someone, I often kept silent, so I winced when my father debated Republicans from business and Democrats from the Center. I understood "unintimidated" before I knew the word, but often felt self-conscious myself, admiring yet fearing my dad's self-confidence.

As I grew older, I began to realize that my father traversed multiple intellectual, social, and political worlds,

regularly blowing through stereotypes since he refused
to recognize their boundaries. His library and periodicals
were wildly diverse; I found myself surrounded by histories,
novels, satires, liberal works, conservative works, Western
religion, Eastern religion, agnostics and atheists, a veritable
great books conversation on our bookshelves. Some were
surprised that he owned these books and read them. My
mother recalled the time they were at a party for Reinhold
Niebuhr, esteemed theologian, ethicist, and political theo-
rist, who was visiting Hutchins' Center. My father admired
Niebuhr for his progressive realism, which sought to knit together liberal ideals with the conservative acknowledgement
of evil in an age of totalitarianism. Bach also appreciated his
serenity prayer:

> *"God, give us grace*
> *to accept with Serenity*
> *the things that cannot be changed,*
> *courage to change the things*
> *that should be changed*
> *and the wisdom to distinguish*
> *the one from the other."*

Chatting with Niebuhr over a drink, Bach suggested connections among several serenity writers, including Zen interpreter Alan Watts, and Christian Science renegade Margaret Laird. Later Niebuhr turned to Hutchins with a puzzled look on his face: "He's a realtor?"

Hutchins smiled ironically: "From the University of Chicago."

He was my hero, however; and while a taskmaster, he was the chief purveyor of fun, always adding a special twist. We played catch every summer evening, no matter how tired he was. He turned every catch into a fantasy game, with a Vin Scully-like narration of my feats at first base following his various pop ups and short hoppers. When we went to Dodger or Angel games, we breakfasted at the visiting team's hotel, so I found myself sitting next to World Series Champion manager Johnny Keane in the coffee shop, or in lobby chairs with MVP Elston Howard. Theater tickets were first row.

"I know, I know," said his ticket scalper when he'd see Bach coming: "She's deaf, she's blind; on the stage she's gotta sit."

When I was twelve, my parents were planning a freighter trip to Panama, but a revolution broke out. They went anyway, the only passengers on the boat. Bach wasn't going to let some damn revolution ruin his vacation plans.

In my junior year of high school, I noticed the Center Magazine sitting on our coffee table. Knowing that Robert Hutchins was Bach's teacher and friend, I read an article of his on the Constitution. Hutchins thought it should be rewritten from scratch.

Rewrite the Constitution? So that's where my dad got the guts of a burglar. The next year, when I had the opportunity to hear Hutchins speak and meet him, I jumped at it, and first heard him express his views on liberal education. So I was primed early to seek out my Berkeley Program and soak up the opportunities at college, and become a teacher. I wanted to pursue my dreams, but one of my dreams was pleasing my father. The man who taught me to seek my own path was consciously or unconsciously beckoning me to his.

My father never asked me to join the family business, but increasingly, if indirectly, he made it sound more and more appealing: Santa Barbara, potentially lucrative, possible serious executive opportunities. Partly intrigued and partly anxious to please, I gave it a try after two years of teaching. He was careful to distance me from him, in an office out of town where I would rarely encounter him. He was sensitive to the obvious nepotism issues, and everyone was polite, but I was obviously "Bach's son," and the youngest person in the company. Worse, I realized after some months how much I missed teaching, and the community of a campus.

I had come to my crossroads. Could I advance confidently in the direction of my dreams without my model's approval, when his approval had fueled me all of my life? And if he withheld his approval, knowing my true feelings, was he a gigantic fraud, claiming freedom for himself but denying it to me? Who was my father when the real rubber hit the road?

"What do you think he'll say?" I asked my mom.

"I don't know. Come for dinner Friday and let's find out."

So I went, and after dinner, fortified by food and wine, I stated my case.

"This is your world, and you know I respect it, but I need my own. I'm activating my teaching file."

He looked at me carefully for a moment without saying a word. It seemed an eternity. This was our whole relationship, about to be defined forever.

Finally he spoke: "Pete, Thoreau says most men lead lives of quiet desperation. Don't be one of those people. Of course you should activate the file."

On the way home, I stopped for a celebration drink. My hero hadn't failed me. My model was still my model. After a few minutes, on a hunch, I stepped into a phone booth and he answered.

"Anything wrong?"

"No. You and Mom wouldn't want to join me for a drink would you?"

A brief silence. They were probably getting ready for bed, a pair of tired sixty year olds.

"We'll be down in ten minutes."

Tonight was my turn to throw the party.

----

Bach in old age slowed down a bit physically, but remained a dynamo, regularly reading *Forbes, The Wall Street Journal, New Republic* and *Mother Jones,* carefully exploring views on the left and right. Living in my childhood home, he finally shot his last basketball hoop at eighty-one, after cracking his wrist with his grandson. Approaching ninety, he watched games, went to concerts, ate superbly and opened wines with Hitler's corkscrew that he had liberated in 1945. Finally felled by a stroke, his last months were spent in assisted living near us in Pasadena. When it became apparent that physical therapy would never make him independently mobile, he quietly, without fanfare, decided to die. He was supposed to pass away within a week but— of course—it took six, with that fierce heart beating firmly. Creating his life up to the end, he oversaw all arrangements. When I assured him that his ashes would be scattered in the Pacific, near Santa Barbara Biltmore, he said: "Good. At least I'll know where to go if I want a drink."

Two weeks before his death, he insisted on a Kentucky Derby Party in his room, sending me to Santa Anita to bet on a hot tip and insisting on mint juleps, even though he could have only a sip. His horse ran out of the money—and may still be running—but it hardly mattered. My father finished his own race, on his own terms.

---

The week following his passing, I met with my father's financial advisor, who smiled when telling of Bach's visits to the office, carefully armed with questions on specific stocks.

"Most of my older clients are in bonds and cash," said Bernie. "Your dad was the only ninety year-old I ever knew who was 80% in stocks."

Always planning for the future.

When we met with his attorney, he said, "Here's the will I wrote, or you might say transcribed, since your father insisted on writing personal messages to each of you into the document."

And sure enough, there he was, hopping out of the stale legalese with his inimitable prose, affectionately teasing each of us while explaining individual bequests. He had arranged regular birthday and Christmas gifts for his grandson for special adventures, because, as he explained to him in the will, "at those times, a guy's got to have a little spending money."

He's still throwing parties.

# DEBATE

There is, of course, a perspective that dismisses my portrait of my program and teachers as sentimental antiquarianism, possessing a certain charm possibly, akin to the gentle clip-clop of the horse and buggy, winding its way gently to grandmother's tea party. It has, this view asserts, little relevance to student and societal needs in the twenty-first century. In a *Wall Street Journal* article on January 3, 2014, Glenn Harlan Reynolds argues:

> *"Today's emphasis on measuring college education in terms of future earnings and employability may strike some as philistine, but most students have little choice. When you could pay your tuition through*

*college by waiting tables, the idea that you should*
*'study what interests you' was more viable than it is*
*today, when the cost of a four-year degree runs to*
*six figures. For an eighteen-year-old, investing such*
*a sum in an education without a payoff makes no*
*more sense than buying a Ferrari on credit."*

And Jon Meacham, in his *Time* cover story of October 7, 2013, notes: "What's fueling the core-standards conversation now is the ambition to succeed in a global economy and the anxiety that American students are failing to do so."

The questions emerging are age-old ones, dressed up in global, technological and post-2008 clothing:

1.  How does one prepare best in college for future economic success?

2.  Is economic success the only reason to go to college?

Based upon surveys conducted as chair of the economics department at the University of Virginia, Sarah Turner concludes that students suffer from "information deficit" regarding the liberal arts and believe three unexamined assumptions: liberal means left-wing, arts means the humanities only, and there are no jobs for graduates. Liberal, of course, means liberty, or, as Hutchins professed, "the arts of freedom." The liberal arts, including the Great Books series, have always included math and science. Hutchins once wrote:

> *"Mathematics is indispensable as an intellectual technique. In many subjects to think at all is to think like a mathematician."*

And both Reynolds and Meacham see the liberal arts contributing to a career.

Regarding the first question, Reynolds admits that "a rigorous liberal arts education, with an emphasis on reading carefully and writing clearly remains a tremendous asset for employment as for citizenship."

And Meacham concludes:

> *"The college graduate who can think creatively is going to stand the greatest chance of not only doing well but doing some good, too. As long as the liberal arts tradition remains a foundation of the curriculum in even the most selective of collegiate systems, there is hope that graduates will be able to discuss the Gettysburg Address…in a job interview at Google."*

Certainly career preparation is a primary motivation for college. But are we focusing too narrowly on our definition of career preparation? Is being narrowly practical the most impractical launch into the job markets of the future? Peter Cappelli, professor of management at Wharton and director of the Center for Human Resources, thinks so:

"For many parents and students, the most lucrative path seems obvious: be practical. The public and private sectors are urging kids to abandon the liberal arts and study fields where the job market is hot right now…It all makes sense, except for one thing: It probably won't work."

Cappelli asks a series of vital questions: Can we predict where the new jobs will be? Is the current data on job placement reliable or misleading? Will overspecialization hinder a graduate's ability to adapt to an uncertain future? Specifically, which degrees from which schools will or will not matter?

He concludes: "If you do specialize, delay choosing majors and narrowly focused courses as long as possible" or "go to college and get a well-rounded education and worry about the job market after graduation."

This from a business school administrator specialized in human resources!

Cappelli's article is particularly valuable as a contemporary analysis, making use of current data and the present landscape. I had heard his central arguments before, however, from Robert Hutchins in 1969 when I was in high school, just as my father had in 1930. Each generation's liberal artists have defended against accusations of economic naïveté, countered with a broader vision of the economic horizon.

But Hutchins, from 1930 until his death in 1977, focused his special attention on the second of the age-old questions: Is economic success the only reason to go to college? Why else might one go?

Hutchins argued that there were three reasons to go to college, since he focused on three components of a complete life: professional, public, and personal. Only a broad-based liberal arts program attended to all three needs. Over the past decade, writers of diverse backgrounds have focused on each feature of Hutchins' trilogy.

Since 2008, much of the liberal arts defense has centered on career. Cappelli and Meacham identified skills, knowledge, and sensibilities that foster success in the work place. A recent article by a Coca-Cola executive detailed the advantages of hiring liberal arts graduates from an employer's point of view. Another study suggests that English majors, after submersion in imaginative literature, developed empathy that made them better negotiators. Financial advisors speak positively about backgrounds in political science, psychology, and behavioral economics, while intellectual property lawyers may stress the need for a science background. A 2014 article by Allie Grasgreen quotes a study, "How Liberal Arts and Science Graduates' Majors Fare in Employment," which argues that liberal arts graduates in their peak earning years make more than their professional counterparts. All of these examples question the assumption that these graduates are doomed professionally, and stress the pragmatism of a broad-based background.

Addressing Hutchins' second theme of public responsibility, academic administrators have bewailed the failure of colleges to produce informed, responsible citizens for local communities and for the American public. Bennington College president Elizabeth Coleman has labeled higher education as "impervious to the health of our democracy," and substituted "self-interest and crude vocationalism" for "a vision of a public life." In 2006, Harry Lewis McKay, professor of computer science and former Dean of Harvard College, raised a stir with his publication of *Excellence without a*

*Soul,* which questions the current purposes of Harvard University, the school he attended and has served for thirty-five years. He has commented:

> *"Universities used to find it more natural to talk about civic responsibility and about the moral obligations democracy imposes on its citizens...Universities have lost some of that old spirit that they were dedicated to the service of society."*

Lewis also turned to Hutchins' third concern, the need for our people to live fulfilled and authentic, emotional and spiritual, lives:

> *"Presidents, deans, and professors rarely tell students simple truths, for example, that the strategizing and diligence that got them into the college of their choice may not, if followed thoughtlessly, lead to an adult life they will find worth living."*

He laments: "The old ideal of liberal arts education lives on in name only. No longer does Harvard teach the things that will free the human mind and spirit". Note that Harry Lewis served as a dean of the college he is critiquing for eight years, and that he is a pioneer of the technological revolution as a computer scientist. Yet he still wants more from the school he loves, and from all schools.

In a similar vein, former Yale University Law School dean Anthony Kronman published *Education's End: Why Our Colleges and Universities Have Given Up on the Meaning of Life* (2007). Kronman agrees that colleges—and specifically the humanities—have departed from their original purpose of conducting Hutchins' "great conversation" about life's purpose in favor of fractured and narrow specialization. He calls for a re-focus of college onto what should be the central question of the college years—and the years to follow:

> *"With wisdom and sobriety and the courage to face our mortal selves: let our colleges and universities be the spiritual leaders they once were and that all of us, teachers, students, parents, citizens of the republic, need for them to be again."*

This from the pen of a lawyer, responsible for training attorneys for a world of practical affairs.

In his 2013 collection of essays, University of Virginia English Professor Mark Edmundson points to the "character

making…dare I say soul making" potential of great literature. He asserts: "It makes you see that life is bigger, sweet-
er, more tragic and more intense—more alive with meaning
than you had thought."

He notes, "You may not have read yourself aright, and
college is the place where you can find out whether you
have or not…The best reason to read great books is to see
if they know you better than you know yourself."

He recalls, "I thought [teaching] was a high stakes affair,
a place where, for want of a better way to put it, souls are
won or lost."

He asserts, "There are simply too many sorts of human
beings, too many idiosyncratic constitutions, for any single
map of human nature, any single guide to the good life, to
be adaptable for us all."

In his 2014 book *The Meaning of Human Existence*,
Pulitzer Prize winning biologist Edward O. Wilson re-affirms
Hutchins' perennial call for a collaboration across disciplines:

> *"We're doing very well in science and technology.*
> *Let's agree to keep it up, and move both along even*

*faster. But let's also promote the humanities, that which makes us human, and not use science to mess around with the wellspring of this, the absolute and unique potential of the human future."*

These recent writers vary in emphasis—and sometimes specific subsets—of Hutchins' three purposes of college education and the life beyond. In some instances, they disagree with one another. I'm less concerned about any differences, and more focused on a common theme implicit in all of their perspectives: Are we willing to use the freedom we possess?

In 1831, French aristocrat Alexis de Tocqueville traveled the young American nation, resulting in his classic *Democracy in America*. He began his journey wondering if such a society would be too volatile, but concluded, by contrast, worrying whether the nation might grow too tame:

*"The prospect really does frighten me that they may finally become so engrossed in a cowardly love of immediate pleasure, that their interest in their own future and that of their descendants may vanish, and that they will prefer tamely to follow the course*

*of their destiny rather than make a sudden energetic*
*effort necessary to set things right."*

In 1848, John Stuart Mill wrote *On Liberty* in his native
England, noting the pernicious effects of cultural conformity:

*"Society can and does execute its own mandates . . .*
*It practices a social tyranny more formidable than*
*many kinds of political oppression, since, though not*
*usually upheld by such extreme penalties, it leaves*
*fewer means of escape, penetrating much more deeply*
*into the details of life, and enslaving the soul itself."*

Mill is championing the confident pursuit of our dreams,
"framing the plan of our life to suit our own character."

In 1965, Robert Hutchins wrote *Education for Free-*
*dom*, arguing that "the liberal arts are the arts of freedom."
It is probable that the most "practical education will prove
to be a theoretical one...what is wanted is the ability to
face new situations, solve new problems, and adjust to
new complications."

All of these writers are issuing high-bar challenges to us, as individuals and as a society, demanding that we hold out for rich professional, public and personal lives. Can we perform this genuine hat trick? Are there examples of people flourishing in our contemporary world to give us the confidence to refuse to settle for lives of quiet desperation, and seek richer, fuller, more creative alternatives?

# PROFILES

*The real story of advancing confidently is embodied in the lives of people who have chosen the bolder path. Like stories of Hutchins, Greenblatt, and Bach, each of the following profiles tells of a highly individual journey of sincere people who refuse to settle for less than authentic self-discovery, practical success in their own terms, and a contribution to the greater good. Every one of them pursued their passions, exhibited strong determination, was a lifelong learner, embraced entrepreneurial qualities, found mentors, had transformational experiences beyond the classroom, and committed to a larger purpose beyond themselves. They are exemplars of Thoreau's dream.*

# MARK KRISS:
## *Constant Re-Invention*

When we were all in the Residential Program freshman year at Berkeley, Verlyn Klinkenborg, now an acclaimed author, referred to Mark Kriss as the "avatar of hip." Indeed, in his unruffled, amiable, calm confidence, his sure taste in art, music, movies and books, his spare, understated but hilarious storytelling, his exotic, well-traveled past, he appeared the embodiment of cool. Whatever space we were all going for, he seemed already to inhabit.

"I grew up in an academic family," Mark recalls, "which was in many ways ideal. My dad was a professor of medicine, and a passionate painter. My mom had her doctorate in family therapy. I lived on the Stanford campus."

His world travels began early, during his dad's sabbaticals in Paris and London before Mark was five.

"I started Kindergarten in Paris, six blocks from the Eiffel Tower, where we'd walk regularly when we weren't doing art projects all day long. It was the most wonderful school you can imagine. I don't want to say it's been downhill ever since, but it was pretty great!"

Bilingual by the time he returned to Northern California at age five, he settled into Bay Area schools, enjoying classes, but having more fun with the student occupations of the Stanford buildings. "My education was as much around the Stanford campus as the high school classroom."

His other education came during the summer between his junior and senior years, when he talked his parents into letting him join friends on a three month trek through Europe—unsupervised, unstructured, spontaneous.

"There were six or seven of us, most of them a year older than me. Sometimes we'd stick together or pair off. Sometimes I traveled alone, hitchhiking through Britain and the Continent. It was inspirational and transformative."

Pretty much done with the idea of high school when he returned for his senior year, he persuaded his parents to let him graduate a semester early, and he headed for Mexico to enroll in an art school in San Miguel de Allende.

"I'd kept up my French throughout high school, but decided Spanish would be more useful, so I took a Berlitz course before I left. It was a counter cultural atmosphere, a great way to gap high school and college."

Mark had a choice between Stanford and Berkeley, and because of his father's faculty status, a free ride to both. He chose Berkeley.

"I don't remember thinking very hard about it. I needed to get away from home. And The Residential Program— small classes, first rate students, great faculty, customized learning—made Berkeley an easy choice."

So Mark, with the rest of us, moved into Spens-Black Hall in the fall of 1970. Devoting most of his time to history and English in The Program, he continued his Spanish and dabbled in painting. During his sophomore year, he decided to become a studio art major. At that time, he had no exposure to technology, or any "future-oriented" stuff. Over the years, he would appreciate that everything he was doing was future-oriented. His junior year was spent at the University of Madrid, another transformative experience.

"There were 80,000 students, so, like at Berkeley, you had to be self-directed. There was a small program for 50-60 kids from all UC campuses, taught in Spanish. The highlight was *The History of Spanish Painting in the Prado*, divided between lectures and regular visits to the museums. I also did some studio work where Goya studied."

By then Mark had fallen in love with Jane Holton, a Residential Program classmate, who would herself become a two-time Visiting Artist at the American Academy in Rome. They spent much of that junior year together in Europe, would return to their senior year at Berkeley, marry and set out to become artists. They both painted following college, preparing portfolios for MFA programs, while Mark earned money building picture frames. Mark applied to multiple schools, and was accepted by...none.

"I was kind of devastated by that," he remembers. "But our consolation prize was a move to Mexico for five months."

Mark did odd jobs, made masks, and prepared a new portfolio. They almost died during the Guatemala earthquake, barely thirty miles from the epicenter. Mark remembers "a harrowing escape, no food, no transport, no contact with family.

"It was a real wake up call, coupled with my second rejection from graduate school. I set up shop in a scrubby little house in Santa Rosa near cow pastures, freelancing by designing posters, wine books—barely scraping by."

Approaching his mid-twenties, Mark had no idea what to do. Eventually he did manage an emerging Sonoma County

Arts Council, but it was hard to sustain with no money. Eventually, he thought of becoming a museum curator, and won a Smithsonian Fellowship at the University of Minnesota. He completed all coursework for a master's in art history, looking forward to an internship at the Walker Art Center—which he failed to get. He was back at square one.

"I didn't know what I wanted. I realized that I had satiated my interest in art criticism and theory. And my options in that field were not that attractive. I noticed the faculty, however talented, seemed a little disgruntled in Minneapolis."

Mark had visions of ending up in some cultural backwater, an art history or museum academic hobo. And he reflected that his artistic interests had taken a new direction.

"I was becoming more interested in the relationship between art and technology. I had researched Baroque water fountains, which were really water-powered robots. And I studied Peter Blume, a painter and sculptor from the thirties and forties, who created an allegory for the introduction of the radio. I found I was gravitating more toward the technology within the art."

Mark had no specific field in mind. But he knew he abhorred anything second-rate. So he re-invented himself on a quest for the first-rate.

"I researched every highly ranked program at Minnesota: Engineering? That would be a tough retread. Medicine? That was a short exploration. Law? No. Then I discovered that Early Childhood Education was top ranked. I thought: I'm not really interested in kids, but that's interesting. Then I saw that journalism was also top ranked that year, for their work on the effects of media on childhood development."

So Mark Kriss went to the dean of the journalism/communications school, and proposed an interdisciplinary master's program. Intrigued, the dean said, "Sure, we'll take you on."

In his late twenties, Mark started over.

"I didn't take one journalism class. I wasn't interested in journalism. But I was interested in mass communications so I took communications research, social science research, statistics, communications law and business school classes in consumer behavior."

Mark commented in a Minnesota alumni profile:

"I think the most interesting thing you can do is combine unusual backgrounds and capabilities. Liberal arts training is a real advantage in that way."

Mark emerged with a thoroughly individualized master's degree, and a background in creativity, analysis and communications just on the eve of the digital revolution.

"Interactive T.V. was just getting started then...and cable T.V. was just expanding. I joined the Yankee Group in Boston, a hotbed of activity providing strategy recommendations, based on consumer research in the pre-internet era."

Mark's specialty was telecommunications and cable networks as electronic shopping was being developed, the Bell Telephone system was broken up, and the future of cable networks was being conceived.

"It was a period of incredible experimentation, with the need to marry tech possibilities with consumer behavior. It required real integrated thinking.

"I'm not a big technical guy—I have a layman's understanding of computers—but I did understand their importance and necessity in these potential markets." In 1984, with a three year-old son and a second on the way, the Krisses returned to Palo Alto to be near family and for Mark to continue more in-depth research at the Stanford Research Institute. There he met Dennis Rohan, a software developer and an early founder of the entrepreneurial program of the Stanford Business School. Fifteen years Mark's senior, Dennis became mentor, colleague and friend, with a track record in successfully starting companies.

The idea of real world application of his research appealed strongly to Mark.

"In the consulting world, the work you do and the recommendations you make are often ignored. We were interested in really tying technology to business strategy."

Mark and Dennis realized that international currency trading was a huge profit center for banks, and potentially a larger one, but there was limited technology for decision making. In 1985 they set up a separate company to create trader workstations using Sun Microsystems technology, and to further develop the analytical capabilities of traders. Ten banks, from JP Morgan to Credit Suisse to Chemical Bank signed up for versions. Mark was the Chief Operating Officer, managing product development, overseeing sales and marketing and general operations. He remembered this time as "intensely stressful but very interesting." By 1989, they had sold the company to Dow Jones.

At age 37, Mark stepped back to assess the past few years. He'd enjoyed a decade of significant success; he and Jane had two beloved boys. And he was initially attracted by a new opportunity in London. In that same year, Mark's dad passed away unexpectedly, causing him to reflect on his priorities.

"I had been running hard for years, and was somewhat burnt out. I realized, *I'm done with my current professional obligations*, and unwound the situation."

For the next three years Mark "retooled," in Palo Alto, spending more time with family, starting a clip-art business with Jane that was less stressful but eventually successful enough to be sold. This latest re-invention allowed him to pause and refresh, so he was ready when his previous partner approached him with some interesting news.

In 1969 the internet, then named the ARPANET, initially connected four computers at universities, including the Stanford Research Institute, Mark's former employer. This was years before home or office computers. In the 1980's the National Science Foundation funded the campus-based internet for non-commercial use. Dennis learned that the National Science Foundation would be phasing out its support in the coming years and the internet was going to become commercial.

Mark and Dennis immediately grasped the implications. They thought, *let's start a new company and become the first internet provider.* "We should buy those campus networks."

Having a track record from their previous success, they were able to raise twelve million dollars from a private equity firm in New York, sharing stock in the new company, and went on the road to study the networks.

The new company, Global Internet (later Comprehensive Technology), eventually acquired the University of Nebraska's network to become one of the first commercial internet providers in the Midwest, but the climate was anything but calm. "It was a wild west land grab," recalls Mark. "I was back and forth to Lincoln, Nebraska all the time. We were inventing everything along the way. Total chaos, a big mess."

But it eventually worked; the company provided internet service and became an early leader in developing network security software. In 1998 they sold the service features to Exodus, the security branch to Cisco.

"I could have gone to Cisco or stayed with the remaining company, but after these years of constant activity, I was toast. Time for another time out."

Another re-invention.

Mark and Jane wanted to enjoy their sons' final high school years in Palo Alto, but made plans to retreat eventually to Inverness in Marin County, and decided to build an environmentally responsible house.

"I always had an interest in home building. So I approached a talented architect, and he agreed to teach me if I would bring him into the digital age."

Mark got a general contractor's license, was draftsman on the project, worked on design, and completed the home for a 2003 move-in. For the next six years, he and Jane worked on their art and enjoyed the quiet retreat. Mark also started a new business.

"I had studied modern portfolio theory at Stanford, and partly out of boredom started an investment management company for friends and family. It was part-time, but I did secure a major trust account I continue to manage today."

In 2009, Mark and Jane moved to Rome for several months as Jane pursued her art at the American Academy and Mark considered his next move. As recounted in a Minnesota alumni profile, he was sitting in the Academy reading Homer. As the profile suggests, it helps if your imagination works like Mark Kriss's.

He noted that even Greek gods got their predictions wrong, and he began to focus on prediction.

"I had become fairly radicalized on the topic of climate change, particularly after hearing at a Berkeley lecture that scientists around the world had even more dire predictions on global warming than was commonly understood. I was concerned that we the public did not know this."

Stepping back yet again, Mark began to conceive his next move.

"My biggest takeaway over the years was that, for me, it was less what you did, but whom you work with and whom you're spending your time with. And whether it's fun and interesting. Our background in interdisciplinary studies gives us the flexibility to think and operate this way. I find this quite liberating."

Mark decided he wanted to work with his sons—Jesse, a music major at Carleton who became a software developer, and Peter, a graduate student in behavioral economics employing precision methods of conducting surveys. And Mark wanted to work on improving climate outcomes.

"We established Vision Prize, a web-based expert poll of 340 climate and earth scientists that created a new opportunity for scientists to convey their beliefs about climate risks and opportunities."

Using a Bayesian method, which suggested that there was a strong enough consensus to accept the ominous findings and create an action plan, the Krisses considered their next step.

Mark explains, "We had three options: attempt to influence the general public, the elites, or the financial markets. I believe that if you can divert capital on a global scale from climate stressors to more climate-resilient alternatives, outcomes will improve. We call this *geofinancial engineering.*"

Mark decided to fuse the activities of Vision Prize with his investment management firm to create Macroclimate LLC, "financial application solutions that incorporate science findings to invest in a low-carbon way to reduce the carbon intensity of investment." Scientifically based social choice investing, in the interests of the planet.

Mark believes that overwhelming scientific data, presented honestly, "not guaranteeing outcomes, because there is uncertainty," can serve investors' interests while protecting the planet.

"We think that we could be a trigger, in a kind of subversive way, to bring that result forward."

The sixty-three year-old Mark Kriss, multiple reinventions informing his vision, has fused his professional, public and private lives, sounding a lot like the eighteen year-old Mark Kriss.

"I'm coming back to my Berkeley roots. It feels good."

## MARK SALZMAN:
*Sincerity*

When Mark Salzman was twelve years old, he saw the movie pilot for the *Kung Fu* T.V. series. He was mesmerized. His future spoke to him from the screen: he would become a kung fu warrior.

"What ignited my interest was not the fighting, not the superhero aspect. It was that he seemed so at ease as a human being, so secure in his own skin."

Mark was struck less by what the warrior did than by who he was: calm, authentic, sincere. Because Mark came from a family of worriers, he writes: "If the Salzman family had a coat of arms it would be a shield with a face on it, and the face would look worried." From a household replete with anxiety, the kung fu master was "the most exotic image conceivable." Mark hungered for his identity, and vowed to become him.

"The idea of being relieved of a chronic sense of anxiety, mostly about the future, was bliss. The warrior was not a superhuman, but a person who learned in a school. There was a curriculum, a body of knowledge, exercises that I could study to develop this ease. He seemed like a boat that has a lot of ballast, not easily capsized—that appealed to me hugely. I was enchanted by a transformation that completely expunged worry or self-defeating thought."

So Mark immersed himself in martial arts, Chinese philosophy, Zen studies, painting, literature. His Ridgefield, Connecticut parents offered ironic and bemused support, hoping the obsession was a passing phase, but noting that he got daily exercise, seemed to be reading a lot of books and stayed out of trouble. His concert pianist mother was a quiet perfectionist, his father more public with his stress.

"If my father heard a soft knock in the car he could reel off a worst-case scenario in seconds: 'the transmission is shot, this will cost thousands.'"

Mark turned his basement room into an Eastern shrine, convinced that he could turn himself into someone who didn't make mistakes, assuming "the breakthrough would come in a mystical, magical moment." By temperament cautious, the kid who said "maybe we shouldn't do that or we'll get into trouble," he was the youngest, the shortest in his class, incapable of drawing interest from girls. Since he felt incapable of keeping up with the herd, he tried this breakout run. For years he studied with a crazed kung fu master, developed skills, sought "purification through pain," and "learned how to take a punch." He read voraciously, not the books in school which he'd study sporadically, but all things related to Asian cultures.

"I took a functional approach to school, taking the tests to get me to the next stage, but I never thought *Tess of the d'Urbervilles* could impact my life; but when I wanted to know something, I read everything about it."

His other sustained commitment throughout his school years was to the cello, which he began at age seven. He showed promise, and considered playing professionally, realizing that kung fu warriors were not guaranteed semi-monthly paychecks. His mother encouraged him without pushing at all, possibly questioning whether he would ever be a soloist.

"My fear of failure in music was much greater than my search for the sublime. Years later, in my thirties, I took a lesson from a true professional for whom I played a Brahms sonata. His advice: "Be more cavalier, Mark. Your technique is fine, but you're too tight. Forget about your fingers.""

Not yet a Zen master in cello.

Fifteen years old during the fall of his junior year in high school, the young warrior/scholar/cellist was getting restless, so he wandered into the nearby Yale admissions office, after hearing that its Chinese Studies program was first rate. On a whim he filled out an application, and sometime afterwards was contacted by an alumni interviewer who agreed to come to his house.

"My mother was giving a piano lesson, so we had to go to the basement. My bed matting was under her harpsichord, my cello in the corner, the bookshelves filled with Eastern literature. He asked me what I was interested in, and I took off."

No doubt the interviewer told the admissions office that he'd found somebody unique, on fire with his passions, wholly self-motivated, completely genuine. In December of his junior year, Mark received a "highly likely" letter from Yale—for the next year.

"I showed the letter to my father, and he said 'are you sure your application wasn't stapled to somebody else's?'"

There was one problem, his father—a social worker—explained apologetically: They couldn't afford it. No problem, Mark thought. He'd graduate early, play music, and get a job for a year, which he did.

"It was a great year. I got an office delivery job—totally non-intellectual, but very social—and felt refreshed for college the next year.

When he arrived at Yale, he noticed that his advisor was the Music Department Chair, which had him worried. He was admitted as a music major and brought his cello, but in the meantime had heard Yo Yo Ma and "knew it was over" (years later Mark would perform with Yo Yo Ma at Lincoln Center).

Apprehensively he told his advisor that he didn't want to be a music major. "Great," the advisor exclaimed. "Now you can do what this college is designed to have you do: taste things. Chinese Studies? You've come to the right place." And in that advisor Mark had found the right guy.

"Yale was fantastic. I sampled archeology, psychology, pre-modern history, English and American literature. I'm glad the breadth of requirements forced me to stretch a bit. I received so much personal attention in Chinese literature—I was the only one in my major in my graduating class."

As a senior Mark worked with a Chinese poet who could barely speak English. As they walked and talked, the poet urged Mark to write down brief thoughts in paragraphs.

"He became the model for my later teaching. The only requirement for that kind of writing is sincerity."

Following graduation, Mark spent two years teaching English in China, where he was popular, but in his own estimate, not yet very good about thinking carefully about his classes. His real motive for being there was to find balance among the Zen masters in their temples by "trying to transform myself into something else." Their message to him: "you can't find what you're looking for by trying to become us. You need to find it in yourself."

So he returned to New Haven as a martial arts teacher, which he terms "a bust."

"I wasn't interested in my pupils' motives: break a neck or move energy and cure cancer."

Mark would often tell a story about his martial arts master from kung fu and a friend suggested that he write it as a story. Mark looked at the first draft and realized that verbal storytelling didn't automatically translate to the written page and worked hard to edit it through multiple drafts. Finally he felt ready to read it to Yale's Chinese literature department chair.

"When I finished I looked up, and he burst into tears. I thought, *wow, this is like a musical performance.*"

Mark had never thought seriously about becoming a writer, but encouraged by initial responses, wrote more little essays on China and bundled them all to an editor at Random House, expecting nothing. He was shocked when she called to say they wanted to buy it. In 1986 Random House published *Iron and Silk: A Young American Encounters Swordsmen, Bureaucrats and Other Citizens of Contemporary China*. In time it would sell over 300,000 copies, be nominated as a Pulitzer Prize finalist, and be made into a movie that earned "two thumbs up" from Siskel and Ebert. Mark thought: *maybe this is what I should do.*

In the meantime he had fallen in love with Jessica Yu, a Yale English major. Following her graduation, they moved to San Francisco, where he wrote under a two-book contract and she experimented with film, first as a production assistant on frozen food commercials.

"Jessica would roll the spaghetti on the fork for the cameras, but at least we were saved from starving by the frozen food left on the set—plenty of waffles."

By 1989 they had moved to Los Angeles, where Mark wrote and Jessica worked on commercials, *West Wing*, and her first love, documentary films, one of which earned her an appearance on Jon Stewart's *The Daily Show*.

The nineties were deeply productive years for both Mark and Jessica. Jessica won the Academy Award in 1996 for her film *Breathing Lessons*, while Mark published a series of successful novels and nonfiction memoirs. He was referenced in *The Los Angeles Times* as "acclaimed writer and certified hipster." He even tried his hand at ad modeling. When he was thirty-seven, he was carded in a La Cañada store while buying a six pack, and in desperation pulled a magazine off the shelf to show the manager: "See, *Time Magazine* thinks I'm old enough to drink," pointing to the Dewar's ad. In 2000 Mark won a Guggenheim fellowship, a mid-career award to those "who have already demonstrated exceptional creative ability in the arts."

The next year, everything changed.

Mark had never wanted kids, but in 2001 the Salzmans had Ava, their first baby girl. Mark remembers:

"When I first held that child in my arms, I was hooked. It was instantaneous. I wanted to spend all my time with her."

The announcement of Ava's birth read: "To hell with writing." Their second daughter Esme was born in 2004. Mark became a full-time dad, doing little writing for several years, not missing it in his preoccupation with his daughters. He published *True Notebooks*, his memoir of teaching in juvenile hall in 2003, but he says that was okay since personal memoir is his "sweet spot." But at that point he felt he'd run out of true stories to tell. For two years he worked on a thirteenth century novel on the Mongol Empire, which he packed off to his editor. Her response was not encouraging:

"Mark, are you kidding? This is awful." Second draft, two years later: same reaction. Another eighteen months, a third draft: same.

"I had no back-up plan. I thought I'd take off some time with the girls and fall right back into it. The harder I tried, the tenser I got, and that set of fears I'd suppressed for so long came rising up. I began having panic attacks."

At the same time, in 2009, Mark's sister grew critically ill, and Mark returned temporarily to Connecticut to care for her family. This period—his own writer's block and his sister's tragic passing—are movingly recounted in *The Man in the Empty Boat*.

"This crisis, and the understanding that those terrors I thought I'd resolved had merely been pushed under the rug, made me realize that they had to be resolved in some abiding way."

The kung fu warrior/Zen temple worshipper had studied giving up control, but secretly thought he was in control because "I was special." One day, mourning his sister's death, unable to write, tending the seizures of a dog he didn't like, he felt at the end of his rope. Suddenly the dog broke wind.

"I exploded in tears and laughter, overwhelmed by the things I could not control. I remembered that when your car begins to skid, turn into the skid to slow the chaos, not against it."

As an extremist, Mark initially gave up the idea of any control, but at a minimum realized that he could not focus on controlling outcomes. Reluctant to debate a philosophy of free will, he says simply: "I need to *feel*, I don't control, because that feeling is a complete release for me. I can't be the centipede always thinking about each of his legs."

Instead he focused on the idea of the Zen archer, who takes his mind off outcomes by focusing on process. As

Mark puts it, western archers often obsess on distant targets, while the Zen archer focuses on developing form with easy, immediate targets, quietly confident that good form is likely to produce good outcomes. Process leads to product—if you focus on process.

In 2013, Mark visited with us at Flintridge Prep, wondering if we were interested in a part-time writing teacher. He feared we might suggest advanced literature, but was really thrown for a loop when I asked, "What about seventh graders?"

He remarks: "That came out of the blue. My chief memory of seventh grade was the day my male classmates destroyed an art studio, sending the idealistic young teacher out sobbing. We never saw her again."

So, somewhat skeptically, he visited middle school classes, and noted the absence of the *Lord of the Flies* brutality. He'd give it a whirl. In September 2014, he took over three seventh grade writing classes, creating prompts for the students to write honest, reflective paragraphs.

"Seventh graders wear no sophisticated masks, and are willing to go with it. Younger people are really interested in the question "how do I live well," as long as you break it down into manageable phrases."

Like a Zen archer.

"If these kids can write authentic, honest paragraphs about themselves at twelve, they'll be able to do it on a college essay when the stakes are higher. All I ask for is sincerity."

A curriculum, a body of knowledge, exercises to develop this ease.

At the end of the year, when Mark Salzman stepped to the podium to address parents and students, the room erupted in applause and shout outs.

"One student keeps writing me paragraphs every week throughout the summer, as if the class never ended. He's a mini me.

"I figured it was going to be a good year. I had no idea how good."

## TOM FLYNN '06:
### *Road Less Traveled*

One day in class during their senior year, a section of the Class of 2006 was wrestling with a particularly complex passage in a reading. One student said:

"Let me take a shot at it, then Tom Flynn can tell us the right answer."

In a roomful of extraordinary talents, the knowing laughter acknowledged the respect that this independent-spirited thinker was accorded.

"I always had ideas about how I saw the world and what I wanted to do that weren't necessarily the mainstream."

One of his convictions, expressed at that time, was his agreement with Tocqueville's observation of Americans during the nineteenth century, possibly applicable to the twenty-first:

"The more men are alike, the weaker each feels in the face of all...he loses his self-confidence when he comes into collision with them. He comes to doubt his own judgment and is brought to recognize that he must be wrong when the majority holds the opposite view."

At seventeen, Tom wrote about Chris McCandless, the fiercely independent, ultimately tragic focus of Jon Krakauer's *Into the Wild*:

"Despite suburban living, Chris managed to retain different convictions. He was an exception, a rebel who refused to follow the rest of America on the path toward intellectual stagnation. Like Chris undoubtedly did, I see our overly litigious society slowly taking all the risk and independence out of life. Therefore I seek risk and independence in the outdoors."

Tom reflects back with a nine year perspective:

"I was struck by Chris's intentionality. He burned a pile of money in the desert. He was all in—committed to living life as he wanted to live it."

Tom had been an outdoor enthusiast from an early age, impacted by trips with his family to Oregon.

"I remember loving camping, skiing, fishing and catching tadpoles. And then my parents ruined me by reading to me about Sir Ernest Shackleton's expedition to Antarctica. I became hooked on outdoor adventure, and the definition of adventure is: you don't know what you are getting."

entire experience was inspirational for Tom. "That summer," he said, "I knew I had to be a conservationist."

The internship led to a two-year fellowship after college with the Outdoor Alliance, a national advocacy group promoting the outdoor rights of all pursuing "human-powered," non-motorized outdoor activities. Tom's major project during his first year was a partnership summit, drawing together one hundred and fifty conservationists, land managers, and policy planners for three days to create a network that could combine and leverage their political influence.

"The centerpieces of the conference were case studies—eighteen success stories of funded programs to forest service non-profits that produced demonstrable results. The big takeaway was our understanding that if we threw a party, everyone would show up."

In recent years Tom has been concentrating his efforts on a regional alliance under the Outdoor Alliance umbrella, building across five states to create effective advocacy.

"Two weeks ago we took twenty-five people to Washington, D.C. for what is called 'communications education.' It's really lobbying training. We met twenty-five congressmen, as well as agency officials."

By the end of 2014, Tom knew he was approaching a growth-versus-comfort crossroads.

"I have a sweet deal right now, living in Boise, with an interesting flexible job. But I feel I've plateaued a bit, and I need another level of credential to get to the policy level that interests me. It's time to step up to the next level. I want to be in the driver's seat on key issues."

As Tom surveys the landscape of the conservation movement, he sees a political and cultural sea change unfolding.

"The Sierra Club, Wilderness Society and their affiliates have done great work getting us to where we are, but they're getting tired. New, younger interest groups see the face of advocacy changing, and stress a different argument and method.

"The traditional argument was often offered in the abstract, whereas we think people must *experience* the outdoors to appreciate it. Empathy. We also need to stress the business benefits to communities, and we need to utilize social media more to meet people in the way they wish to be engaged. I want to be part of modernizing the conservation movement."

Tom believes his confidence in his decisions has mostly served him well, and that he's always tried to set long term goals. To that end, in his moment at the crossroads recently, he characteristically chose growth over immediate comfort. In August, Tom will enroll in University of Vermont Law School, taking advantage of its renowned environmental law courses, and earning a joint master's degree in environmental policy. He's stepping up. But he'll keep his hand in the outdoors, completing a major mountain biking trip throughout Idaho before he moves, and planning winter visits to his father in Wisconsin, where Tom holds a share of stock in the Green Bay Packers. In 25 degree below zero weather, with winds howling and snow flourishing, he goes into the wild of Lambeau Field.

"The environment is a uniquely American issue. Public land is such a direct democratic process. There you learn to live with less in nature—and elsewhere."

Tom reminds us that the stakes are high and the time is not limitless.

"They're not making any more relatively pristine places. We need to protect what we have."

# CHRIS LINICK '03:
## *The Resolute Dreamer*

People discover their dreams at different times in their lives, creatively experimenting through their 'twenties,' or even finding their vocation at forty. A certain few, however, know their passion quite early and proceed undeterred, if not unchallenged, in the path they have chosen.

"Something about my family encouraged me to pursue science," says Chris Linick. In fact, everything about both parents' work pointed in that direction. Chris's dad Dave enjoyed a forty year career at the NASA Jet Propulsion Laboratory (JPL) in La Cañada, managing deep space antennas that communicate with satellites far from earth.

"My dad is very modest, and didn't talk about work unless asked. I had to pull stories out of him. But I saw early that he had an engineering mind, a very scientific approach to things."

Chris's mom Sue manages teams that run instruments on the Cassini-Huygens spacecraft. So JPL has been another home for the family—for Chris's and his older brother Justin's entire lives. Justin is at JPL now, working with scientists to collect and analyze data on volcanoes. Yet there wasn't a single instance where Chris was pressured to study science. "My parents have always encouraged me to follow my own path. They just want me to be happy!

"That being said, how could I not be inspired by seeing my parents contribute to something so fascinating? So of course I was hooked on science at a young age. It had to happen. There are many other passions in my life that could have pulled me in—music, traveling, cooking, sports, and anything outdoors—but it has been my greatest dream ever since I was a kid to go into space and unravel its mysteries. I have been chasing it for ages—and by chasing I mean doggedly following it all over the place, recklessly at times. We live in a huge universe of unknowns that is vastly unexplored and full of weird things like black holes and exploding stars. That thought of this alone gets me every time. How could I not want to be involved in that?"

"When I finished sixth grade at Saint Mark's School I looked seriously at several schools, but had a magical feeling when I came onto the Flintridge Prep campus. Other schools seemed more structured, but at Prep it seemed like you could bloom in your own way. I enjoyed the entire curriculum. I loved fiction, and cited *Great Expectations* just the other day. But my main loves were math and science."

When Chris graduated from Prep he received an award for being a go-getter science student, but he distinctly remembers being surprised when his name was announced because he had never made any attempt to set himself apart in science. "I never thought of myself as being different or more accomplished in science than anyone else. I just put my head down, worked hard, followed my passions, and it led me there."

Chris opted to accelerate in math prior to entering in seventh grade, and completed Calculus BC before graduating. He also enjoyed all sciences, physical in particular, and by the time he applied to college, he was looking at engineering programs. His final choices came down to Northwestern and Berkeley.

"I was strongly drawn to each of them. I loved the feeling of Evanston, loved Michigan Avenue in downtown Chicago, and respected Northwestern's fine engineering program. But my father framed the argument in mature terms without being invasive: "Where do you want to be in 10-15 years?" He did encourage me to put reason before emotion, and the quality and reputation of Berkeley's engineering were hard to beat, but emotion played a part. I loved the open culture—the blue-haired woman with the dog holding forth in the restaurant, a symbol of Berkeley, of its philosophy of "own who you are and be the best you can be." I have always actively sought out this style of education since it suits me so well. By choosing Berkeley, I had the most room to mess around in the science sandbox, but at the same time, I recognize that this choice meant I had to take the initiative to shape my learning. No one holds your hand at Berkeley, as you know well. It was the harder path for sure, but it was the best for me and my career."

He chose Berkeley, loved it, but found the engineering deeply challenging. "You have to earn what you get at Berkeley. You won't be force fed." As a freshmen he found himself in the "weeder" math course, which had a twenty percent attrition rate. "The grading in engineering was brutal, but all the little scars were worth it."

Most importantly, Berkeley favors the proactive student who seeks out professors beyond class. Chris knocked on the door of a chemistry professor whose teaching he really respected. He became a great mentor for him and employed him as a research assistant for almost two years.

"This chemistry professor was a big role model for me. He was a dynamic, passionate teacher, and I admire how hard he strives to reach every one of his students. I think he indirectly demonstrated to me the high value of education."

Another formative experience happened during the summer following Chris's junior year in college when he pursued an internship at a small research institute in Heidelberg, Germany, which cemented his desire to pursue a doctorate in aerospace, and led to a later internship in Munich, where Chris had an opportunity to fly a spacecraft. He was hooked, and in the fall following graduation from Berkeley, he entered a doctoral program in mechanical engineering at the University of Texas in Austin.

"I was a bit of a wandering vagrant in science, but I was determined to learn how satellites were built, how to launch them into orbit and learn from them."

Within the Cockrell School of Engineering at Texas, mechanical and aerospace studies were both pathways towards Chris's goal, and upon encouragement from a professor,

Chris transferred to the aerospace program during his second year.

"The program was a steep incline, in breadth and depth. I was so focused on my goal that, in retrospect, I realize I had no motivation for what I regarded as obscure formulas requiring mere memorization and regurgitation that had nothing to do with my research project."

Unfortunately for Chris, and the other students in his program, each doctoral candidate was required to pass three detailed written exams prior to focusing on a specialty. In his third year, Chris deferred the exam, but, along with all of his classmates, failed the exams in the fourth year. In the fifth year, he passed two but failed the third. A portion of his fellow students actually passed this last time, but several didn't, including one of his closest friends.

"My mentor said that concerns were brought up in a department meeting about the difficulty and the outcome of the exams. There were three separate professors with no oversight designing the tests, apparently in a rat race to design the hardest question. Science is supposed to teach you a way of thinking, to prepare you with a skill set for original research. These exams did not test for this quality of thought at all. Ironically, they were anti-academic. The professors didn't care about the archer's mark in the distance. They built walls where there didn't need to be walls."

When I saw Chris in 2012, he had reached a crossroads, and a crisis of faith. His dream was still alive but the particular path seemed to be wrong. Five years ago, when he was torn between returning to Germany or going to Texas, Chris told me a doctorate was essential for his work and he reaffirmed that point again, but his runway was flawed.

Seeking to gain perspective, Chris returned to Germany to conduct research. Then an opportunity presented itself. He realized that most of his units for PhD study could transfer to the Department of Geological Sciences at Texas. He would shift gears to intermediate ground between science and engineering with a new geologist mentor with deep connections to aerospace. The doctoral exams would be comprehensive orals with four professors, with an emphasis on his research project. "Not a 'gotcha' thing, but a reasonable, rational process testing your ability to think as an original scientist." Chris's goal would remain the same but the path would be different.

"My story is about not liking the conditions I found myself in, and opening new doors to make the dream work. I took one on the chin with a weird devotion. Maybe I should have taken a step back at twenty-two. I was so focused on my end goal that I jumped pretty quickly...But after eight years and a couple of twists and turns I'm on the right path. I should have my doctorate in the next year."

And after that?

"Not a professorship. I love teaching and have really enjoyed those opportunities, but I don't want to be one of those three guys trying to design the toughest questions. Those exams were lacking perspective, and I feel that a place like NASA offers more possibilities and wiggle room. NASA appreciates and nurtures talent. I've been in this field for a while and done a lot of research. I think I have something to contribute."

At a time when the perfectionist impulse leaves many students risk averse, cautious about trying a new solution to a math problem or an out-of-the-box paper topic, Chris Linick is a reminder of the value of persistence, resilience, steadfastness in pursuit of a dream. He has not been and will not be deterred.

Chris was a varsity golfer while at Prep, loving the competition of a close match. In his final major golf tournament at St. Andrews in 2005, Jack Nicklaus rolled in a birdie on the last hole of his fifty year career, and looked totally unsurprised. "It never occurred to me that the ball wouldn't go in," Nicklaus remarked. People with that attitude make a lot of putts. Or launch a lot of satellites. Satellite projects are often decades or more in the design and execution, requiring patience, optimism, and resoluteness. Chris Linick has found his calling.

## MEGAN KIMBLE '04:
*Empowerment*

During my sophomore year at Berkeley, my apartment mate Walter, impoverished from his imaginative but expensive spending habits, went looking for work. One day he struck gold, securing a dishwashing job at a newly opened neighborhood restaurant. In addition to providing rent money, this gig also supplied housemates with late night snacks, as Walter sometimes smuggled leftovers on his way out the door. One night he brought chocolate mousse. The first bite was confusing, tasting nothing like the sweet milky bars commonly found on store shelves. After the next few bites we realized it tasted like...chocolate.

Who made that mousse?

His boss, it turned out, a woman named Alice Waters, who opened her new restaurant, Chez Panisse, to bring to Berkeley the same dining experience she'd discovered in France: fresh, seasonal ingredients, grown locally, eaten leisurely among friends and loved ones. Food, as she famously said, is a way of life.

The rest is history. After more than forty years, the "mother of American food" has shaped not only how we can eat, but how we can live, after concluding in 1971, a time of apparent chaos and helplessness, that we have the choice to take control of our lives, one carrot at a time.

---

When Megan Kimble was seventeen, she wrote:

"The way I am able to get up and out of bed every morning is to believe, to know, that I am free and that I have the ability to change my life. I have hope in and for my future; I hope that I will have the strength to walk my talk, to stand up for what I believe in, to stand alone in a world that doesn't always support my stance."

When she was twenty-seven she wrote:

"Some challenges, like global warming, feel so insurmountable that it seems as though nothing can be done. But we live in a world of insurmountable obstacles. When we do things without small specificity, without localness and precision of place, it is hard to ask and harder to answer: What do we want to change and how do we want to do it?"

Pausing between readings during the book tour for *Unprocessed: My City-Dwelling Year of Reclaiming Real Food*, Megan reflected on her time at Flintridge Prep:

"We did a huge amount of reading, getting a true canon in high school. I'm grateful to have read those books so young. And writing, when you weren't allowed to fail, but had to work to get it right."

During her freshman year at the University of Denver, Megan was surprised to find some students indifferent to their classes, having grown up in a culture of engagement, both at home and at school. But by the time she talked her way into advanced writing classes, she hit her stride.

"They were workshops, so we read each other's work, guided by some amazing professors. I also wrote for the school newspaper, and eventually became a section editor, which I loved."

Her on-campus journalism led to two "hugely important" internships, one with a city paper, and another with a publishing company, giving her real life experience in different facets of the information world. By the time she graduated, she knew, as she had always suspected, that she wanted to be a writer. She also knew she wanted to see the world. A semester in Argentina had given her the travel bug, coupled with a senior seminar on Che Guevara, whose boldness struck Megan. She writes of the advice given to recent college graduates:

"Be bold. But I didn't really know how. I wondered: Does boldness exist only in military fatigues? Could it also wear a sundress and flip flops?"

After college she moved to a small fishing village in Nicaragua, earning free housing in exchange for English lessons.

"It was so disorganized," she says. "My planning consisted of, "Hello, I'm here teaching English, please come." After five months, I found a more formal job in Grenada, and went back and forth between village and city. Throughout that year, I lived a lot more simply. In the evenings, people passed the time by sitting on their front stoops, all in a row. No cell phones, and there were periodic electricity outages. And for a year I could eat only what was given to me—no choices."

Once the novelty wore thin, Megan faced the discomfort of an uncertain future:

"I didn't know what I was doing with my life. I thought, *I'm teaching, but I'm not trained to do any of this. I want to be a writer but I'm not really writing.* I remember struggling."

Megan came home and lived with her parents for a year. She was a substitute teacher and coached basketball. Her memories of Nicaragua "flamed something in my brain," and she worked nine to five writing a cultural and economic history of the nation. It remains in her computer. She applied to thirteen Master of Fine Arts writing programs, and was rejected by all of them.

"I had an absolute meltdown. I didn't know where to turn next. I was devastated."

Because of this crisis, she began working every network she knew and eventually landed a position at *The Los Angeles Times*.

"*The Times* was transformative. I learned about the industry and about writing. Having pieces published in *The Times* made me so much more confident as a writer."

Almost as an afterthought, Megan "threw out two apps" to graduate programs she respected, not expecting anything. She was accepted at the University of Arizona.

"It was the most intense writing experience I've ever had. I used to meet people and say, 'I'm trying to be a writer.' At Arizona, I said 'I *am* a writer.'"

As Megan put it, she "hit the ground running." In a small, writing workshop of thirteen, she explored the craft of writing, and delved deeply into the research component of quality journalism.

"If you want to know something, you don't go to Wikipedia; you go talk to experts and study primary sources. You learn what question to ask as you become deliberate about what you want to find out."

In graduate school, Megan took a variety of courses, from science and geography to nature writing, integrating her work from diverse fields as she "learned how to focus [her] attention on the environment, climate change and food.

"I'm curious about how the world works. I don't know how the world works, and I want to know more."

Megan wrote a short article about processed food, which prompted her to dig deeper. She had always been interested in food, growing up with parents who were vegetarians who paid attention to the food industry. She learned to cook at home, and from an early age was deliberate about the selection and preparation of food.

"I went through phases: vegetarian, carnivore, dieter. My friends and I cooked diet food, baking with Splenda. Terrible concoctions."

As Megan began to understand the impact processed food has on both her own health and the health of the environment, she felt overwhelmed until she met Kimber Lanning, director of Local First Arizona. Kimber's mantra: SPEND MONEY BETTER.

As Megan writes: "Our dollars have the power to change the way things run, and yet we give them away with such ease.

"What if we pushed our economic levers deliberately and purposefully? I remember the Montgomery Bus Boycott, when Martin Luther King, Jr. and others urged African-Americans to refrain from riding to cost the bus company three quarters of its business. Buses were integrated in a year. We can vote with our feet and with our discretionary dollars. Empowerment. As Kimber Lanning says, 'empowering the American people so that they can see that we are the economy'."

So Megan decided to start not only locally, but person-ally. She would spend a year attempting to eat only unpro-cessed foods, recognizing that most food has undergone some processing, but that an apple was different from a bag of chips. And she would write about it, exploring the im-pact of her decision not only on her health and diet, but on her social life, and on one's ability to find "a different way to live urban life."

Megan was encouraged by a professor to use her gradu-ate workshop as an editorial board, so while her classmates were submitting separate articles for peer review, Megan submitted book chapters.

"I knew I wanted to write narrative journalism, so this was a perfect opportunity. I've never wanted to write personal memoir, but this was my story, so I needed to weave me into it. My classmates always challenged me to be more candid."

While eating unprocessed and working on her book, Megan became interested in *Edible Communities*, the net-work of local food publications, and wondered "why isn't there an *Edible* in Tucson?" So a professor introduced her to a publisher and she became a founding magazine editor while still in graduate school. The girl who couldn't find any opportunity suddenly had every opportunity.

"I got an agent in New York, who put me through a crash course on book publication: Editors liked the book but complained that I didn't have enough "metrics"—blog hits, Twitter, social media visibility. So I posted online for months, secured a book contract and advance from William Morrow."

When I met with Megan, she was preparing to fly to New York and New England for the next leg of her book tour. She's encouraged by the early reception of *Unprocessed: My City Dwelling Year of Reclaiming Real Food*, and will meet with her publisher to discuss her future.

"I am first and foremost a writer, interested in food, but wanting to find something new to learn about eventually."

Mostly, Megan is captivated by the concept of empowerment and the conviction that her generation will create change as "the little things begun on our own" grow in impact. As she ends her book:

"Because, really, all you can do is begin."

Just ask Alice Waters.

## RACHEL TOBIAS '07:
*Fearlessness*

Rachel Tobias always did things a little bit differently.

"I was the kid whose socks didn't match...they still don't. I've always tried to push back on what was the norm."

So what led to the sense of adventure and fearlessness? Her father was an entrepreneur for whom risk was a daily reality, and her mother was fanatically devoted to international travel, making sure her children were exposed to new cultures and experiences from an extremely early age. When Rachel was nineteen, she saw a globe with an emphasis on Africa and South America. Today, she wears a necklace with the same image. During the five years following her high school graduation, she studied in Egypt and spent a year working in Indonesia. Through it all, her parents supported her, even when her choices seriously challenged their comfort zone. Not that their opposition would have stopped her.

"I was never very good at heeding warnings—especially if I felt the advice was coming from a place of fear
rather than reason."

Fearlessness. Rachel has never been daunted by new
challenges. Indeed she seeks them out, and gets restless if
her current circumstances become too comfortable.

She fondly remembers her high school experience at
Flintridge Prep and the constant "feeling of excitement
about learning.

"I learned how to be curious, how to ask questions. I
had rich relationships with teachers, who taught me how to
think critically, how to think creatively. I was taught to be a
strong writer, which has served me extremely well today."

Rachel's Great Books final paper is a testimony to her
critical and creative thought. In it, she pairs seven different
wines to seven different philosophers, explaining how the
wines' properties reflected the essential qualities of the authors. For example:

> *"Aristotle is Axios, a dark firm Greek wine, with earth,*
> *currant and cedar, mineral notes representing the*
> *strength and standard which Aristotle stood for.*

*Plato: The Boutari Naoussa Grand Reserve. It is rich, complex, with an excellent structure. Its long-lasting aftertaste reflects the immortal mind of Socrates and his ability to continue his teachings long after his death. With Freud we have the 2004 Fruner Valliner Alte Reben Kremstal—a clean, crisp wine which tends to have a more complex and deep fruity aroma."*

Rachel's most significant memories of high school center on the relationships she formed during that time: "I've sought and maintained regular contact with high school teachers as well as other mentors. My parents were strict about insisting that I have conversations with other adults who came into our home. It was considered rude not to. The ability to carry out conversations with adults and peers helped me to approach new relationships and new friendships without fear."

Did she ever submit to unthinking, imaginary fear in high school?

"The college search. It was devastating. I convinced myself that there was only one school for me: Georgetown's School of Foreign Service. I spent a year completely anxious pursuing that goal and felt destroyed when I didn't get in. There was no reason for despair. My parents never put pressure on me. In fact, they hoped I'd stay in Los Angeles. I caused so much unnecessary agony for myself throughout this process. What I didn't realize at the time is that college success isn't about where you go, but the experiences you create for yourself while you're there. The key questions to ask are about the opportunities that college provides. Are there interesting internships available? International programs? Can you get personal access to your professors? Is the university located in a place you want to explore or in a community you want to get involved in?"

Rachel enrolled at the University of Southern California, partly because of the Honors Thematic Options Program featuring smaller humanities classes. She enjoyed it, but quickly began to explore the boundaries of the university.

"I didn't want the typical undergraduate experience—I felt compelled to push back on what others were doing, to push back on the norm. I opened up my world in ways that didn't confine me to campus."

Soon she found herself interning at the school's social entrepreneurship lab, fascinated by the blending of private enterprise and social impact. And she began to study Arabic.

"Some people raised their eyebrows at Arabic. But I never wanted to fit into a box. I liked it when people raised their eyebrows."

Her next step was a semester abroad in Cairo, Egypt. Given the cultural and political tensions that surrounded her, in particular being a woman in the Middle East, she sometimes felt overwhelmed.

"I was nothing short of ecstatic and excited about studying in Cairo, probably in a somewhat naive way. There were times that were emotionally and physically difficult, and psychologically uncomfortable."

She was not too uncomfortable to refrain from traveling through the Middle East, sometimes alone as a young woman; nor to neglect a later opportunity to volunteer in China; or take a summer internship in Washington, D.C. By the time she graduated with a degree in International Relations in 2011, she had cobbled together a richly textured cosmopolitan experience. She joined two valued mentors in a Los Angeles startup company, where she worked for about a year, until she was offered a fundraising position at a school in Indonesia.

"To a fault, I am almost obsessively open to new opportunities. I never want to live with regrets."

While Bali was a good learning experience, after about a year Rachel decided it wasn't the right fit for a long-term role. So in the summer of 2012 she found herself back in California taking my summer Great Books class when she received a call from IDEO in Palo Alto, a global design consultancy co-founded by David Kelley, also founder of the Stanford design school. I had studied Kelley recently myself, seeking guidance for our school's own IdeaLab, intrigued by his method of combining engineering with a human-centered, deeply client-based collaboration. I was thrilled when Rachel took the job.

"I'm in a business development role, helping bring in new projects, managing relationships with new and existing clients and mediating between the project team and the client. There are two main components, in my opinion, that make our work cutting edge. First and foremost, design-thinking methodology, which is really empathy work for the people we are designing for. When our clients ask how they can be more innovative, we help them better listen to and understand their customers and uncover what they actually need. We do observations, interviews, put ourselves in the shoes of our users as a way to discover latent behaviors and needs that can inform the design of new products and services. For example, early in my time at IDEO, we were hired to help improve the design of a net-zero army barracks. As a team, we spent several nights in the existing barracks to better understand the day-to-day challenges of a soldier's life in these barracks, and uncover potential opportunities to improve the design. We tried to better understand the culture and listened to their stories. We then spent three days with a large group of enlisted army guys, collaboratively prototyping new solutions and features of their quarters. It's amazing what happens when you give people a voice. These eighteen and nineteen year old guys, many without high school diplomas, immediately became transformed when they were invited to participate in the design process. At the end of the workshop, they said things such as: 'I think I want to go back to school to become an engineer. I never knew I could build or design things.' They learned that anyone can create meaningful experiences or products. Listening builds great confidence and self-esteem.

"The second thing that differentiates us is that we are very fearless about sending ideas out into the world. We're a culture that asks for forgiveness rather than permission. Rough, rapid and right prototyping defines our design process. For example, one weekend an intern decided to build a treehouse in the outdoor patio of our workplace. He didn't ask anyone, simply bought wood and equipment, and when people showed up Monday morning there was a brand new treehouse. People still have lunch and meetings up there. We're empowered to make our own decisions and to take risks without a fear of failure. A motto is: fail often and early. It's OK to throw initial plans away. Don't feel like everything is precious."

Twenty-first century ideas reminded me of an early twentieth century character. In Shaw's *Major Barbara*, a play Rachel and I had read together:

> *"What do we do here when we spend years of work and thought and thousands of pounds of solid cash on a new gun or aerial battleship that turns out just a hairsbreadth wrong after all? Scrap it. Scrap it without wasting another hour or another pound on it."*

Rachel continued. "A colleague and I are very concerned with sexual harassment on college campuses, so
we're exploring how we might start to solve these problems
in this country, without necessarily having a specific client
that is paying us to do the work. We haven't asked anyone's
permission. We're just going for it."

Rachel has clearly found a home.

"When you get to work with this caliber of people with
such deep empathy, consulting with such an array of clients,
it's hard to think about working anywhere else."

So what's next? What's the emerging vision?

"I'm not sure what's next. I'm personally extremely passionate about the Olympics, and how we might help the
Olympics achieve more economic and social impact. The
current I.O.C president is very progressive, calling for things
like multi-country hosts in the future. What if the Olympics
were less of a tourist-centric moment in time and more of
a driving force for international change? That's a project I
would love to work on."

So at age twenty-six, elementary school world traveler,
the high school girl with dreams of foreign affairs, the col-

lege international student, extends her global landscape to the most ambitious levels, fueled by the empathic creativity of her current work.

"I never want to settle in a job just for the money, where I don't have impact. I want to live a life I'm proud of. And I don't want to miss anything."

## NAOMI HATANAKA '11:
*The Balanced Bubble*

When she was seventeen, Naomi Hatanaka asked herself in a paper: "What could possibly intertwine the humanities and physical science?" Her answer: equilibrium. She explained: "A good life is an overfilled balloon at the brink of popping because it is so full of experiences and energy. What keeps the balloon from popping is the equilibrium that is reached between birth and death, an individual's reconciliation of her fantasies and real passions." Since that day, Naomi's life has been a search for equilibrium, a balancing act of discovering and pursuing her multiple passions without bursting.

A key characteristic of Naomi's is her ability to immerse herself completely in the moment, while remaining aware of long-term dreams. "I came to Prep because it seemed less about end results—grades, college—and more about opportunities to explore. In my early years I loved biology, and was immediately attracted to the beauty of the Spanish language. But my outlook on life really changed during the summer following sophomore year, when I underwent yoga teacher training."

For Naomi, yoga became the gateway to self-study. She sought opportunities, through yoga, meditation, and reflective walks, "to calm the fluctuations of the mind," in her case, a mind threatening to explode creatively in multiple directions.

"Eastern philosophy is about opening yourself up, being receptive to everything you are shown. This opened up my world in high school, and changed the way I thought through problems."

During the summer between her eleventh and twelfth grade years, Naomi was shown an entirely new world, when she and her classmates accompanied their Spanish teacher on a homestay trip to Nicaragua.

"For years my mom threatened to send me to a third-world country. She worried that I didn't appreciate my home, school or the comforts of our lives in the U.S. that we take for granted. In Nicaragua I saw a different pace, lifestyle, culture. I saw people making $1 a day with no job security, shacks with roofs built from street signs, orphans begging for money outside of our restaurant while we complained about the marinara sauce. It was an eye opener for very privileged people."

Most impactful was time spent at La Mascota Hospital, a pediatric cancer center serving Nicaragua's poor.

"My father had cancer so I was used to the hospital—but ones like our Keck Center. La Mascota was bare; colored walls but not uplifting. Families slept outside after traveling long distances for their children's treatments."

Naomi talked extensively to the patients and their families. She learned that many families who lived outside of Managua found it impossible to secure transportation into town for their children's regular treatments, and had no place to stay. She began to understand that children in Nicaragua were dying for lack of access to healthcare.

"When we returned from our trip, my classmate Kyle Eschen, my teacher Señor Nuñez and I asked a simple question: What was the root cause of unnecessary death? What were the issues we could tangibly help solve? We agreed that our focus should be logistics."

Naomi understood that further research, medical training, and increased healthcare funding was important, but those were macro long-term issues. Most immediately, specific young cancer victims needed immediate, ongoing

treatment, but they had to get to the hospital to receive
it. Available transportation would save lives. Further, $50 a
month—to us she points out, "a nice meal," would provide
food, soap, oil for cooking and a month's transportation for
an entire family. Her fundraising appeal: "$50 saves a life."

Naomi and Kyle vowed to create something beyond a
transitory effort by a couple of high school kids momentar-
ily affected by a trip. During their senior year, Naomi began
plans to create a California Foundation with 501(c)(3) status.

"We wanted a long-term commitment, offering tax breaks
to donors and to the foundation. We felt a legal entity
would be recognized as more legitimate and would validate
our cause."

As a sophomore, Naomi had been a student with the
Pasadena Independent School Foundation, an organization
devoted to teaching youth philanthropy. She approached its
president, who walked her step-by-step through a foundation application form. Her teacher, Manuel Nuñez, was her
advisor and contact with La Mascota Hospital. Her mother
Sara helped with business and legal issues.

"I've always been comfortable approaching adults,"
Naomi commented. "My mom placed me in adult situations

when I was very young. I loved to talk with parents about what they'd done with their lives. And I've been close to many teachers."

What should be the name of the foundation? Naomi and Kyle considered Fugacidad, which suggested a certain fleetingness to life, but they agreed that it might be too dark. Naomi notes, "You can't really sell that one." They had recently read *A Room of One's Own*, Virginia Woolf's account of material necessities lifting one's spirit, and of a character who finds her truth within. A possible link between yoga and Nicaragua? They decided to call the foundation A World of One's Own. It received articles of incorporation the next year.

When it came time to select a college, Naomi had a clear idea of what she was seeking.

"I wanted a totally different experience from the small private schools I had attended all my life. People had handed me my schedule and spoon fed various structures since kindergarten."

She chose Berkeley. While she strongly felt the transition from Prep where students receive extensive attention from faculty, she grew to love it for its size, its progressive tradition, and its diversity. She loved the fact that knowledge was being created every day throughout the campus, and that she could work with original researchers. "It's an honor to be taught by these people."

During her freshman year, Naomi pursued a true liberal arts curriculum, distinguished by its breadth across many departments. From Spanish literature through cognitive science and psychology, she searched for strands that tied her intellectual journey together. Eventually she majored in interdisciplinary studies, with an emphasis on social entrepreneurship, global development, and urban and regional policy. With such a diverse major she had to appeal her way into most classes.

"You need to be able to email total strangers and state your case in order to take a class. I had to talk myself up a bit, which is hard to do. Berkeley taught me how to be scrappy."

Friends wondered why she didn't enter Haas Business School and focus on more pre-professional courses. They wondered if she would ever find a job. Her interests, in and out of the classroom, seemed so widespread. She was executive vice president of the Pan-Hellenic, coordinating programs for sorority/fraternity education in sexual assault, alcohol use, health and empowerment. After enjoying her Introduction to Entrepreneurship class as a freshman, she contacted her professor to offer her services, and ended up as the teaching assistant for the class during the next three years.

"All of those experiences gave me confidence. Sometimes you build confidence by practicing assertively. Public presentation requires you to project confidence even if you don't have it. I also had powerful role models in strong women. All of these experiences built my leverage point. Everybody needs a leverage point, some perspective other than 'here's how to cut costs.' A breadth of knowledge and experience gives one a leverage point. Mine is social responsibility."

Between her sophomore and junior years, during an internship in Washington, D.C., Naomi was invited to a Deloitte Consulting Impact Day. Their offices were open spaces, free-flowing, reminiscent of a Silicon Valley company. She was dazzled by the breadth and depth of their projects, and when she eventually interviewed for a job, was pleased that they were interested in her background.

"There's no way I would have gotten my job without my leverage point. At Deloitte I noticed that you make a contribution to your team with your unique perspective. I haven't taken accounting, and know only a little Excel. They want you to be somewhat of a blank slate so they can teach you best practices that they have learned from their clients. That philosophy gives you a lot of freedom in what you can study."

So Naomi ended up with the job those more narrowly focused students wanted, partially because of her varied background, her obvious love of learning, and equally apparent ability to learn.

"People place so much pressure on themselves to get jobs and sometimes get it backwards. I remember a story from my Hindi class that suggested focus can help but only one focus can blind you. I strongly agree that the back door is often the best door in."

So Naomi received her offer from Deloitte during her senior year. She's excited about being a team member, perhaps in a small group of four or five, perhaps in one of fifty or one hundred in a "big Silicon Valley divestiture." She knows she will work hard, but Deloitte emphasizes work / life balance which she will need, since she still has A.W.O.O. for La Mascota, and a new socially responsible coffee company she has founded with a friend. Her balloon seems close to bursting, but she understands equilibrium, and she understands herself.

"I've never really been focused on what I'm 'supposed' to do. My model is my late dad, who was groomed by his family to be a doctor, but gave it up to follow his passion as a music teacher. My mom is the person I go to for practical and personal support. I learn to my capacity, annotate all my books carefully, and I write thoughts on my own. I'm not ready, like Prospero in *The Tempest*, to drown my books yet, because I haven't internalized it all yet, but they're on my shelf."

As she wrote at seventeen: "I'm on my way."

## CAROLYN TING '03:
### *Head and Heart*

Each morning, when I pick up my coffee cup at work, my eye is drawn to the coaster with the following quote:

> *"We are such stuff*
>
> *as dreams are made on."*

I think of Shakespeare, but I also think of Carrie Ting, who gave me the coaster over twelve years ago. Prospero's soliloquy demands attention from both our heads and hearts, and is an apt gift from Carrie, who sometimes suspects she is a romantic, but knows that reason and emotion are dynamically balanced in her identity and in her dreams.

"I was looking for a high school with top academics, but kindness is something I've always valued, so when I heard that Prep was looking for 'nice people, good kids,' I thought I found a place where I could learn analysis but also explore other parts of myself: my heart, my soul."

During her high school years, Carrie was a top student in all fields, but particularly attracted to courses with an interdisciplinary approach, such as ninth grade geometry, taught by a St. John's Great Books graduate, and courses like Spanish Literature, which blended culture and philosophy. She also liked "Prep's emphasis on giving back to your community, which was important for me to hear at an early age."

In the spring of her senior year, when she had whittled her college choices to UCLA and Berkeley, Carrie realized that she faced a defining decision.

"It was a classic comfort-versus-growth situation for me. UCLA was the safe option: great school, local, near my grandparents' house, where I knew I'd be happy. Berkeley was initially intimidating, but with an energy I'd never experienced before. A place that would be difficult but rewarding."

Whenever students come to visit with me about college selection, I try to ask questions without giving a recommendation. I do suggest multiple coin flips, not to make the decision, but to discover what the "heart" might reveal.

"When you stood up and flipped that coin, I wondered, *what's Mr. Bachmann doing?* But I knew before the coin hit the floor how I wanted it to come out.

"Berkeley was the perfect stepping stone in my life, where all these diverse voices sat at the table. The atmosphere helped people and empowered them."

Carrie enrolled with the intention of being pre-med, since a doctor struck her as the perfect combination of head and heart and empathy. She found the science classes pretty cutthroat, however, with students expressing mixed and sometimes self-interested motives for pursuing medicine.

"I realized, 'I really need to want this,' which prompted a lot of soul searching. I began to understand that you can heal people through many avenues. I also learned that doctors often treat patients one-on-one, and I wanted to impact healthcare on a larger scale, perhaps, at the program and policy level."

So Carrie double-majored in business and psychology, combining analysis and "the human element." She also studied comparative literature and continued her Spanish, which led her to a study abroad program in Spain during her junior year.

"Spain was important because I was very much 'the other' in that world, and learned how to assimilate into another culture. It gave me empathy."

Other crucial experiences were summer internships. Her first was in the business office of the Peace Corps, doing both mathematical analysis and personal interviews to uncover reasons for cost differentials. Her second internship, in management consulting, resulted in a job offer and led to a three plus year stint as a consultant.

"Consultants sometimes consider themselves the doctors of business; getting to sample multiple types of businesses with different problems. You also learn to listen deeply.

"At Deloitte Consulting, I started in a rotational program, which exposed me to strategy, finance, and operations across multiple industries. I didn't know exactly what I wanted to do, but these experiences allowed me to test hypotheses. I always knew healthcare was an interest."

Carrie was intrigued by the world of philanthropy, but was cautious about joining any non-profit that might be insufficiently focused on safe outcomes and limited by restricted financing.

"I learned to be wary of unintended consequences, and decisions made too remotely from the community and community leaders in question."

Was there a philanthropy that attempted to combine rigorous business practices with large scale healthcare impact?

After three years at Deloitte, Carrie was offered sponsorship to enroll in an MBA program cost-free—if she returned to Deloitte afterwards. At the same time, she was offered an opportunity to become a program officer at the Bill & Melinda Gates Foundation in Seattle. Another defining decision.

"The MBA was the rational decision. Deloitte was a great company. It was a safety net if I wanted it. But I wondered, 'what would it be like if I found a more natural fit?' Should I risk making assumptions about my passions? I had internal confidence, but what if my gut was wrong?"

Being a good business student, Carrie created a financial model replete with detailed assumptions and variables that quantitatively analyzed the potential financial outcomes of each decision. She determined that she was likely to lose $500,000 if she took the Gates Foundation job.

"I presented my findings to my scientist father, who studied them, listened to me, and finally used non-scientific criteria: He said that if after doing this analysis I still wanted

Gates—if that choice means so much to you—I should do it. I did the analysis, but then went with my heart."

In practical terms, the Gates Foundation proved to be a good strategic decision. It had enormous resources, with a broad focus on global health, development and education. Carrie started on the strategy team in the global health program, applying business acumen to philanthropic decision-making.

"Bill Gates loves data, and he wants to understand how data informs your recommendations. Even the Gates Foundation has limited resources, but it is big enough to make different bets on different horses. You can afford more risk with a larger portfolio."

The Gates Foundation provided Carrie with unparalleled opportunities, with her desk just feet away from renowned experts in various fields. She traveled to Uganda, Rwanda, Ethiopia and China, learning on each project to think a bit out of the box, respecting history but not necessarily accepting it as a perfect blueprint for the future.

"When I joined, I was one of the youngest program officers at the Gates Foundation, younger than the historic job requirements. If I had bet on what had come before I

would never have gotten the job. I've always been comfortable in places—Prep, Berkeley, Gates—that have spread-
sheets but aren't afraid to break the mold."

After three years at Gates, Carrie again took stock of her
dreams, her strengths, and potential liabilities. She knew
that global health was her passion, that she'd had invaluable
experience throughout her twenties, but knew also that she
might have perceived limitations. One of them, ironically, could be my son's uncontested assertion that "she's the
sweetest person in our class."

Carrie has reflected on this issue:

"I'm a nice person, come off as a nice person, and can be
perceived as lacking strength. I look for mentors who know
my internal strength, believe me when I say I can do the job,
and provide me air cover in certain rooms. I want a seat at
the table, and need the authority and credentials to get there."

Carrie determined that she needed a graduate degree
and considered three options: medical school, an MBA or
the newly emerging Master's in Management.

"After all these years, I circled back around medicine,
even though it was late in the game. The old health re-

gime was dominated by doctors and researchers. But why would I go to medical school not to practice medicine? I would be seeking a medical degree with the intention of shaping global health strategy and impact. So I bet on the future, following my heart but also my head, that the private sector and business will be an increasingly important factor in healthcare."

So she faced another defining decision. When she called me to have lunch she was down to two options: a two-year MBA at MIT—the conventional, safe choice, or a four-quarter accelerated Master's in Management at Stanford's Graduate School of Business.

"The Stanford program could be a risk," Carrie said. "It's not as universally recognized a program, but it may have long-term advantages. First, it's designed for senior professionals, with experience. And secondly, it has a thread of behavioral economics rooted in psychology spun through the curriculum. I wanted to understand how feelings and emotions influenced decision-making, in addition to rational analysis. Even at Gates I found that decisions were made with more emotion than people realized."

"I don't think we need the coin flip," I said. "You're on the cusp of a decision."

"I really want the Stanford program," she said.

So once again, as with Berkeley and Gates, Carrie played the longer odds. Ironically, because she came from the non-profit sector, Stanford sponsored 80% of her program tuition costs, demolishing the assumptions in the elegant financial model she had prepared for her father three years before.

After two quarters at Stanford, Carrie was bullish.

"My classmates are older, with more humility. They've had big successes and big failures, and are willing to talk about both, making the conversation richer. Much of the curriculum overlaps with the traditional MBA, with finance, accounting, marketing, ethics. But you can 'choose your own adventure,' and mine combines design thinking, inno-vation, health and entrepreneurship. I'm betting there will be demand for this kind of program."

So what's the next defining decision?

"Do I go straight to starting my own business, or work for other entrepreneurs first in a smaller environment than

Deloitte or Gates? I still trust my gut, which at the moment tells me that I may need more experience to break up my intuition. There's been plenty of trial and error, but the mark has become clearer: helping people through global health. Intuition is phenomenally important but not always right. Information and experience reduces the gamble. Stanford is another tool for my toolbox. Another way of thinking to make my passion real."

So Carolyn Ting sharpens her analytical chops, putting a cool head at the service of heartfelt dreams. Akin to Prospero on my coaster, she seeks practical wisdom with a poetic imagination. I like her bet.

## DEBORAH ABELES '96:
*The Archer's Mark*

In the late 1990's, when we were discussing the possibility of a new performing arts center at the north end of our campus, I asked a group of college age alums to analyze school priorities. One of them was Deborah Abeles, who, as a top scholar, athlete, and musician, commanded particular attention.

"Performing art has to be your top priority," she said. "It provides the deepest leverage for your investment. Academics and athletics can be improved incrementally, but enhanced arts facilities and instruction significantly change the school's reputation, attract different girls to Prep to complete co-education, and draw a broader variety of guys. It's your biggest breakout run possible."

I took this analysis to the Board of Trustees, commenting that I thought a nineteen year-old had just outlined our next strategic plan. The rest is history, as we opened the Randall Performing Arts Center with enhanced faculty in 2000.

When Deborah read Aristotle, she approved of his focus on the "archer's mark." She has spent her entire life setting ambitious goals and achieving them. When asked to explain her view of the good life at age eighteen, she identified three priorities: appreciating every moment, striving for excellence, and loving family and friends. Like the true archer, she has taken aim at all three targets throughout her adult life, and seems to be hitting them.

She started shooting her arrows early. In second grade she began the violin, shifting to cello in third. She says she came to sports "late," at age ten, beginning with soccer and moving straight into softball. She always liked school, finding classes interesting, and never needed academic motivation.

"Time management became second nature. I have always felt that I needed more time, but you can't control time."

By the time she arrived at Flintridge Prep from Crestview School, she was a two-sport club athlete, a youth orchestra cellist, and an accomplished student in all subjects.

"Prep was a great fit for me. Great teachers, challenging academics, a fantastic enriching social environment. I definitely benefited from the small school atmosphere. I always preferred the literature classes. I liked math, but I was never real science-y, which worried me since I thought of becoming a doctor. I was very idealistic about medicine: I wanted to help people, and thought nothing of possible social prestige. Initially I wanted to be a vet, but I couldn't watch animals suffer."

Deborah was a college recruit in both softball and soccer, and a potential standout cellist, if, her longtime teacher kindly admonished her, she would only practice a bit more; but "she understood my commitments." She continued to excel in school. Discovering her three areas of passion early, she pursued them ardently through high school, spurred on by her genuine enjoyment.

Approached early by college coaches sitting in the stands at big tournaments, she realized softball was her primary strength, although she continued to play soccer and considered playing both in college as she entered her university. She had many choices.

"If soccer had been priority, I would have gone to Yale, but I really meshed with the girls on the Harvard softball team, who became 'best friends for life.'"

"Harvard was a fantastic four years. I have not one single regret about my choice. I knew as a freshman that I would explore medicine. During the first week my pre-med advisor asked me what I was interested in, and I candidly said English. He said, 'If you have personal interests, now is the time to explore them. If you wish, major in Russian literature. You don't have to major in biology.' I thought, *OK I won't have to spend all of my time competing against physics majors.* That was the best decision I ever made."

Her own father, a chief financial officer of banks and universities, said, "I love to hire English majors, because they know how to write." In addition to majoring in English, Deborah decided to minor in Spanish, which became a passionate love. Playing softball for four years she set records in hits and runs batted in, and was selected for induction to the Harvard Varsity Hall of Fame in 2015.

"Between English, Spanish, pre-med courses, and softball, I was pretty busy. I left my cello at home, and by sophomore year, I decided not to complete all pre-med requirements in four years. College offered too many rich opportunities that I didn't want to miss."

After graduation, she worked in a lab at UCLA and completed the remaining half of her pre-med courses. After additional work in the lab and time for travel, Deborah was ready to commit to medical school.

"I was still convinced that medicine was the place where I could help people. My parents remained encouraging as always. They believed medicine would be good for me from a personality standpoint. My father, a successful businessman, did not believe I would find business fulfilling. I'm more emotional than my dad."

Deborah entered USC medical school, which, in various phases, would be her home for most of the next nine years. During her first two years, she took general courses, uncertain of a future concentration. In her third year, she followed a four part rotation through special fields: general, trauma, neurology, and orthopedics. She found the experience invaluable:

"Medicine teaches you to take nothing for granted. I've seen many people on the worst day of their lives. But people are grateful that I'm trying to help them."

In her final medical school year, she applied for multi-year residencies throughout the country, willing to move anywhere, but hoping for California. She got USC. Residencies are notoriously grueling experiences with brutally long hours. By this time Deborah was married and ready to have children.

"In residency, you drive through patients as quickly as possible. In a class of ten residents, I was the only female. It was not politically popular to have a baby, but the resident director had seven kids so he couldn't really say anything. I scheduled my vacations for childbirth, twice during residency."

Residencies are difficult for single men, but for a married woman with two children?

"It would have been impossible without the support of my family, who have always placed their children first: when my dad was CFO of a major bank, he would regularly clear his calendar for our games and concerts. My mom, a full-time teacher, chauffeured and supported three girl athlete-musicians constantly. So when our babies were born, my mom devoted herself to their care, along with my husband, whose teaching schedule allowed him afternoon and summer time with the children."

Deborah decided to be an orthopedic surgeon. She had been helped through shoulder injuries herself, and loved to see injured people brought back to full health. Her specialty would be foot and ankle, and she was offered a one year fellowship in Baltimore for extra experience. However, her husband didn't teach in Baltimore, nor did her parents live there.

"We faced a family decision. I was looking at having a full-time fellowship and an eventual practice with two babies at home. My husband decided to become a stay-at-home dad."

Deborah's husband, Jaime Castaneda, was born in Mexico, one of eighteen children. His journey to California and his achievements as a teacher and coach have required an unimaginable level of resilience and grit that daunts even the remarkable Deborah. He combines the toughness of an accomplished athlete with the sweetest of natures. He coaches and teaches through positive reinforcement. Deborah says simply, in massive understatement, "He's a very good person, and a very good father." Jaime's commitment to the family made Deborah's career possible.

The fellowship was more relaxed. Deborah was able to follow four doctors around for a year, observing the practice of medicine. She saw four different styles of patient care, bedside manners and interactions with families and staff. It was a great completion of her formal education. As she prepared for private practice, she reflected on her decade-plus of paying dues to become an independent doctor:

"You have to want to do it yourself—not for parents or peer pressure. It's a hard, long road, and if you do it for the wrong reason you'll regret it."

Returning to California, Deborah joined a practice in Southern California. While she still has much to learn after two years with her group, she knows the kind of medicine she wants to practice:

"I take longer with patients than other doctors, and longer in preparing my notes. I want eye-to-eye contact with a patient, and won't ever type on my computer with my back to a patient. I really enjoy the practice of medicine—on most days!"

I remembered Daniel Pink's prediction that the growth of digitalized information, where we can find much of the data we've sought from doctors by ourselves, will make the human side of medicine more important, not less. If true, Deborah Abeles is ahead of the curve again as she has been all her life, clear on her archer's mark.

"I'm still so early in my career, learning the most productive use of my time. Family is most important, and I'm fortunate that my husband agrees and is happy focusing on the kids for the moment. Who knows about the future? I'll be revisiting some questions in ten years."

Deborah sounds unintimidated by this prospect. She knows that she can adjust her archer's mark, as she has done all her life, firmly rooted in the values she articulated at age seventeen: gratitude, excellence and love.

## VASU SARMA '89:
### *The Ambassador*

Over the years, whenever I've asked Vasu Sarma about one of his classmates, he unfailingly delivers a detailed update. And at reunions, I see him visiting seamlessly with actors, athletes, scholars, the shy and the outgoing, with equal comfort, a versatile ambassador among disparate personalities.

"I had my own ambassadors when I was in sixth grade, before I got to Prep. Alex Durairaj '86, a family friend, went to the administration and said, 'This is my friend, and he's supposed to be here.' Since I completely flubbed the interview, I needed the help."

Vas enjoyed his six years at Prep, and is currently a seventh grade parent. "I remember being treated respectfully by anyone I came into contact with. Our class grew extremely close over the years, and it was decidedly normative to include everyone in all events. We grew to appreciate everyone's individuality, and developed an enduring camaraderie."

Vas came from a medical family and especially enjoyed biology, but was also an enthusiastic participant in humanities and history classes.

"One edge I brought from Prep into college was writing. I tried to make it coherent, pointed, with a little bit of flair."

He may have just described himself perfectly.

"I started at USC in biology and gravitated to gerontology as I became increasingly interested in neuroscience. There was a lot of scientific change in that field at the time, and much original research was being done at SC. Gerontology was very well funded to study the differences between pathology and normative aging. My fundamental question was always the same. What does it take to be human?"

Spoken like a true liberal artist.

Vas, however, had another passion in college for the martial arts, to which he devoted major time, until one day when he sat down with his academic advisor.

"I showed him my grades, and asked if I could get into medical school. He answered bluntly, 'Anybody can get into medical school, but not like this. If you want to go, either leave the country or shoot yourself. You're not bringing it to the table. You're doing everything possible to sabotage yourself. Martial arts? Are you ready to work?'

"I'll do whatever it takes. Just show me what to do." And he did, but it was a little late. "If you're looking for someone who didn't take the right paths, that would be me. As a result I was admitted to no medical school in the fifty states. I thought: What have I done? I was depressed beyond belief. When you're thinking of mistakes it doesn't get any more profound than this.

"I was the one Indian kid nobody feared. The Indian or Asian kids walk into the room and people think, he might be a contender. Not me."

Did he consider any alternatives to medicine?

"Yes. I thought of taking a vow of poverty. Perhaps earn a doctorate in neuroscience, hone my martial arts skills, and become a warrior philosopher. But I felt the calling: just get me in front of a patient. That's what I wanted to do."

Vas was accepted to the American School of the Caribbean. His mother, a distinguished cardiologist, was aghast, until she learned that one of her favorite students had gone there. She gave her somewhat reluctant blessing.

"The medical school was on the tiny island of Montserrat, next door to a farm, where you could hear braying donkeys and chickens being plucked. We arrived with fifty in our class, and were down to forty-seven by the third day. By the end of the second year, we were down to thirty-five. If you flunked a class, they kicked you out."

Vas's breakout run began in his third year, which he spent doing core clinicals in England, where he was trained classically and formally in a strict school of hard knocks.

"I'd have my hands literally slapped in the operating room: 'don't cross the field of the surgeon.' I learned to study degrees of formality and expectation, to understand the importance of knowing your audience. I began the path to undo the stigma of going to a Caribbean medical school."

Vas's exams and grades—and the fact that his mom was on the faculty—got him to USC for his fourth year of rotations. He was eventually accepted at USC for his residency. He spent much of those years trying to understand what other people wanted, beginning with the nurses.

"One day an influential veteran nurse watched me fumbling around trying to write orders. I finally said, 'Will you help me?' She put me inside the mind of a nurse, illustrating what it is the other person looking for. What does a patient want to know, and how does he want to hear it? I learned the face-saving difference between saying, 'You missed the bus' and 'the bus left you.' A lifetime smoker and his family don't need lectures on past behavior. They need a clinical care plan, including the patient's view of minimally acceptable outcomes."

While a resident, Vas secretly yearned to be selected Resident of the Year, still searching for "a big undo of past mistakes." He didn't get it. He got something better. In his third year, he got a Distinguished Teacher Award—the first recipient in six years—and was elected to Alpha Omega Alpha, the medical school honor society. Redemption.

Following his residency, Vas was awarded a three year fellowship in pulmonary care and eventually trained in lung transplants, which helped him to understand cardiac surgeons and their expectations. In 2004, he took over the cardiovascular critical care unit at Kaiser.

"I take care of people who've had heart surgery. Patients call me by first name and have my cell phone number. People say thank you when you take your time with them. I also tried to understand the doctors, and became an ambassador for the cardio surgery program to the rest of the hospital. They needed someone to fill the communication gaps and put a good face on cardio surgery. It's essential to bring disparate groups together because when you're not talking there's a problem.

"I appreciate Kaiser's innovations. Their integrated model is relatively unparalleled, combining insurance, medical groups and hospital care, and it was built from the ground up, so everyone is on the same page. We spent $4.5 billion on the electronic records system, and everyone thought we were crazy, but any doctor can open any patient's file. We're not incentivized to hospitalize a patient to collect from an insurer, because we are the insurer. And our preventative care outcomes for chronic care diseases are tops."

Yet, as Vas will admit, his life is hectic, with periodic understaffing and underfunding, a minimal threat to patients but unhealthy stress for medical staff. At the same time he found himself drawn to issues beyond his unit.

"I served as chair of the hospital critical care committee, on other hospital committees, and as board chair at my children's elementary school. I found myself increasingly a facilitator among multiple constituencies, and also a participant in policy level discussions."

So Vas found himself in his mid-forties, at the height of his clinical career, blessed with a loving family, increasingly in demand for civic responsibilities, deciding to go back to school.

"I wanted to leverage my ability to transition to my other great interest: solving problems on a bigger scale."

The Harvard master's program wants to produce clinicians who understand financial constraints. So Vas signed up for a degree program three thousand miles across the country, leaving family and work for up to three weeks at a time, while maintaining all of his usual responsibilities.

"I love it. I wasn't sure about the money part, but financial management, cost accounting, assessing the value of a project in a hospital is fascinating. Now I come to a clinical situation able to look at it from multiple perspectives. If I can come back to Kaiser and tell people respectfully that there are restraints and priorities, they trust me. I'm not just a suit, nor just another clinician."

He's an ambassador.

"I'm also studying organizational behavior, strategy, and the social, community, and political factors that can influence a hospital. I can help colleagues understand changes coming from the Affordable Care Act and Medicare, and appreciate that there's plenty of uncertainty ahead. But the moment you can deconstruct unnecessary mysteries, people relax. We live in a world of 'TLAs'—three letter abbreviations—that poses as elite language only a few people can understand—language other kids can't. Playground politics creates barriers. I try to imagine what I would want to hear if I were in the other person's position."

Vas finds time for other interests as well. The mentor who told him to shoot himself has become a trusted friend, and the two have engaged in annual debates on philosophy and religion, with the "loser" footing dinner. His best friend and most trusted advisor is his wife Sabena, a shrewd business and political analyst who helps him assess the risk and benefits of committing to situations at work, or in private life.

"We first met at a Latin dance club. I was outfitted in the brown suit, the black shirt all open, and the gold chains. She asked me: 'As a calculation for meeting someone new, was that a good gamble?'"

Having set that wardrobe in the rear of his closet, Vas is ready to imagine his longer term future.

"I'd really like to be in charge of Kaiser or some hospital system, or possibly a front line clinician having an audience with the people who make major decisions. At the moment I'm trying to create a platform that keeps all my options open."

Vas is at peace with the idea of complexity, understanding that in most issues there are competing viewpoints, and problems with, at best, imperfect solutions. In hospitals and at Harvard, Vas studies seemingly impossible challenges, and knows that his desire for impact at high levels is deeply competitive.

"There are lots of sharks in those tanks—other people astonishingly accomplished. I'm prepared to meet people who are my betters at every single level. But there's room for all of us to create influence."

Vasu Sarma has come a long way from the braying donkeys and chickens being plucked, always leveraging his talent and work ethic with an uncanny empathy to bring together those people in any room he occupies. With his courageous midlife return to school and outreach into the community, he's just beginning to imagine the rooms of his future.

# BRYAN DENTON '01:
## *The Adventurer*

On the morning of September 11, 2001, Bryan Denton awoke in his New York University dorm room, a recent arrival at Tisch School of the Arts, following his June graduation from Flintridge Preparatory School. As he looked south toward lower Manhattan, he saw what looked like smoke. Soon he discovered that the World Trade Center was collapsing from a series of terrorist attacks. He grabbed his camera, and as others fled the scene, he ran directly toward it.

"It was an instinctual thing to go to the site. I knew it was important. It was my first coverage of a news event, my first photojournalism."

It was not the first time Bryan had moved in one direction while the crowd moved in another. Since childhood, through high school and college, and into his thirties, Bryan had almost instinctively reacted in opposition to the dominant culture.

"What's defined who I am—I've always switched perspectives frequently and drastically. Reacting against the looseness of Sequoyah School prior to high school, I thought I wanted to be an aviator. I visited Army and Navy Academies, but my mother finally put her foot down. No way. Then when I arrived at the more formal Prep, I headed for the most informal place on campus: the art studio. I needed the photo lab; it was my outlet."

He had begun photography in a summer class prior to ninth grade, and at that point, without imagining any specific purpose or themes.

"I just liked taking pictures. It was unquantifiable fun, with a ton of possibilities. I felt very free."

At age twelve, Bryan saw the movie *White Squall*, about an ill-fated sailing trip for teenagers on the open sea.

"I was obsessed with that movie, and depressed for three days by its outcome, until my mother told me to snap out of it. But mostly I was consumed with this idea of going on an adventure. I felt there was more out there."

Bryan was always planning to go places. Each spring he'd research various out of town experiences for the summer. His parents encouraged him, but made him do all the planning and arrangements. The experience helped him to adopt a very practical approach toward realizing his dreams. To this day he operates like a chess player, imagining three moves ahead, a shrewd combination of intuition and careful analysis.

"All of us in high school were raised for a rigorous academic tradition, with expectations of college and career. I enjoyed my time at Prep. The education was spectacular, the best thing that happened to me in terms of a liberal arts background."

By his senior year, Bryan understood that he analyzed best through the lens of a camera, capturing an idea visually. For his Great Books final, Bryan took a photograph to pair with each of the seven philosophers he studied as a metaphor of a central point of view. He imagined his own life picturesquely:

"I am a nomad, set to wander the high seas, hike the Rockies, sell sunglasses in Florence. Once I've adapted, it's time to move on...but I'll still take my memories with me."

Bryan knew he wanted to study photography, but didn't want a pure arts college, so he chose NYU's Tisch, with its liberal arts component, hoping that the broader environment would help him figure out what he wanted to do with his varied interests.

"I'd always loved history, growing up on those *Time/Life* books, where photography contributed to my interest. And eleventh grade American was my favorite. So after 9/11, it seemed natural to take a course in Middle Eastern history. At the same time, to satisfy a language requirement, I began studying Arabic."

So Bryan began to imagine an integration of his interests in photography, history and Arabic for his next logical step:

"I didn't want to do a clichéd semester abroad—Paris or Florence cafes with classmates. So I ended up studying in Jordan, where I did a bit of freelance photo work. That semester in Jordan was everything—without it I would have been too scared to gamble and go back when I was twenty-two."

Upon graduation from NYU in 2005, Bryan found himself with a crossroads decision. He knew he would pursue photography, and that the safe bet would be to take a staff position in the U.S., possibly with potential to work abroad some year in the future. Or, he could roll the dice, move back to Jordan immediately, and work where he wanted to be, doing what he wanted to do.

"It's about taking the right risks. As my Latin teacher, Dr. Mack said, fortune favors the bold. Risk big, win big."

Risk takers, of course, must be resilient, ready to accept setbacks and learn from them, appreciating them as growth opportunities.

"I've failed a lot. Failure is a huge part of doing anything independent or creative. I've had many opportunities to fail. You run against the wall, get up, and try again."

Of course, Bryan chose to go back to Jordan, even though he had no secure employment, knew few people, and faced grinding poverty. He found some freelance jobs with the news service he'd worked with during his semester abroad, but he scrapped by for rent, even in a tiny $150 per month apartment with no toilet. He did find a social network for international photographers, which landed him a *New York Times* story on education. Yet in 2006, he had thousands of dollars in debt on his credit cards, $300 in the bank, and minimal prospects. Then Israel attacked Hezbollah fighters in Lebanon. Desperate to get in on the action, Bryan bluffed his way into a major career acceleration. Even though he had no prospects or plans, he e-mailed the *New York Times*.

"I told them I was booking a flight to Beirut and could help them if they needed me. *The Times* responded: consider yourself hired…contact us when you get there."

But getting there was no easy task, particularly for someone with no experience in the logistics of travel into war zones.

"I started to panic. I had no clue what was expected of me. I booked the one flight available the next morning, made it on the plane, began to taxi down the runway…and we were grounded."

So what next? "I'd heard of people driving through Syria, but since bridges were being bombed, taxi drivers wanted $500. I'm cash poor and tapped out on credit cards."

So he did what any boy does when things are desperate: he called his mother.

"She's in her pajamas, getting ready for bed, and I say: Mom, you need to wire $1,200 *right now*, I'm working for the *New York Times* in the biggest moment of my career.

"She starts crying, saying that if she sends the money and I get killed she'll never forgive herself. I say, 'Mom, if I miss this assignment, *I'll* never forgive *you*."

She sent the money. Bryan moved to a southern sub-
urb of Lebanon, where he witnessed bombings on a daily
basis. Was he afraid?

"Young journalists do stupid things. They're not afraid
yet. Danger doesn't compute at 23, when your neural chemistry is not yet developed. I had no self-preservation instinct.
I was still basically a teenager with credit cards."

So Bryan covered crisis after crisis in the Middle East:
Egypt, Libya, Iran, Syria, rarely "parachuting in," usually "setting up shop" in sites, hoping to fathom some of the enormous complexity around him.

"The Middle East as it is covered is highly misunderstood.
As journalists we're not doing something right. The only
way is to live there, so it seems more three-dimensional,
especially the truth in the grey areas."

Bryan is not ideological, seeking with his camera to
record the facts. He tries to get to know different people,
trusts his instincts when he's filming, then reflects during
the editing process on any overarching themes, organically
weaving his pictures into a story that seems true. He rarely
finds simple narratives, still less often the moral purity he
feels many Americans demand.

"Moral purity has never been interesting to me. I don't think it exists. The people cutting heads off are also looking for moral purity. I find diversity interesting—it's what makes art, literature. It makes us a better species. Even in high school I was drawn to diverse friends: the hippie, the country western guy, the pretty boy Valley guy, all pursuing different interests."

And is he still a nomad?

"I consider myself more of an immigrant. Nomad sounds too romantic. Young people ask me about my work because they seem to find it glamorous—travel, danger, other lands. But they don't seem interested in the work, which I think is important but not glamorous. And places like Syria can get sinister, with rebels a mixed bag of motivation. It's an arena of despair."

Bryan seems tired. Passionate about his job as a true journalist, in the tradition of Walter Cronkite, seeking the facts. Shorn of romanticism, he resolutely pursues his calling, devoted to the search for truth as captured by a camera and edited by a thoughtful liberal artist.

Would he ever come home to America? Such a question asks Bryan to ponder his identity carefully. Born in Pasadena, he lived in this country until he was twenty-two. But for almost a decade has lived in the Middle East, is at home in Beirut, is married to a Lebanese woman. He found a recent assignment in North Dakota (his first domestic shoot) "more foreign than Baghdad." Returning to New York would be "like moving to a foreign country."

Two years ago in a school assembly, when asked if his identity was American, he said he didn't know. But if his national identity is ambiguous, his personal identity is not. He has followed a calling true to his earliest instincts and experiences.

"Some people use sports to find themselves, some the military, some art. I have built those opportunities to define myself. I have nothing left to prove. Now I want to create things I really believe in—stories I find fascinating that haven't been told properly."

Bryan springs forward from this strong sense of self, buttressed by "an incredibly robust support system: family, friends, mentors, love—people who believe in me."

He thinks that young people underestimate the "robustness" of their support systems, and falter in pursuit of callings they love. They also underestimate the horizon of the future.

"The new economy is much more elastic, informal—a million opportunities. Kids have to develop a new definition of success. This economy presents alternatives."

Advice to current students: "Your 20s are yours to do with what you want. The decade is a gift to you. You can fail in your 20s, find something in your 30s and still be fine."

Any concessions to his 30s?

"I'll keep doing this as long as I'm alive…but I may try to downgrade the level of white-knuckle chance."

## SCOTT STUDENMUND '08:
*The Virtuous Patriot*

It was a warm spring evening in 2006 in South Pasadena. Our mission was clear. As part of the Sophomore Retreat we were competing in a scavenger hunt through the town to uncover the hiding place of history teacher, Mike Mullins. Clues were to be found up and down the streets. Our team leader, Alex Jacobs, had a plan: calm, calculated, methodical, which we all began to follow—except one of us.

Scott Studenmund broke into a sprint, turned the corner and raced up Fair Oaks Avenue, intent on out-racing every other team to clues. He got so far ahead of us that he had time to stop for a burrito while we caught up. Once we did, ours was the first group to find Mike Mullins. As his friend Morgan Brown noted, "Scott lived every moment of every day with blazing fire in his eyes."

As a young boy at Clairbourn School he raced around campus. In baseball he raced around the bases, as his mother Jaynie noted, "Fast and fearless. He loved to tear it up."

He also loved to read.

He first read Plutarch with his father in the third grade. He relished history courses always from elementary school through the teachers who inspired him at Flintridge Prep. When he found an author he enjoyed, he'd devour him voraciously. During his senior year at Prep, when author James Ellroy participated in a Q & A, it became obvious that Scott had read all of his books. He was the most well-versed student in the room. As Jaynie observed, "Books were a great way for him to be in his own world." Multiple officers and soldiers commented on his intellectualism.

He was always a warrior, his juices flowing at the sign of competition of all kinds. In kindergarten he loved soldiers and sailors and ships. When he was in second grade, Jaynie, then a senior executive at First Interstate Bank, explained to Scott that her bank was likely to be bought by Wells Fargo. Scott had an alternative:

"Why don't you buy them?"

"We don't have enough money."

"Well, get together with another bank and buy them."

"I'll tell our bank president and CEO your idea."

That night Scott came racing home. "Did you tell him?"

Scott Studenmund, age eight, ready for battle against a corporate takeover.

By his junior year in high school, he started on the football team as nose guard, a position, Jaynie notes, "That played to his personality." It appealed to his "warrior spirit," and it brought him his first band of brothers. He loved being on teams, from scavenger hunts to sports to the military, and relished the closeness of shared effort and accomplishment. His close friend, Trey Kozacik, recalls, "Scott's personality was infectious. If he was laughing, it was impossible not to laugh with him. If he was mad at something, you were mad, too. His passion and enthusiasm alone could motivate people to do things they otherwise wouldn't...It might sound a bit weird, but Scott could also be a calming factor. He had that aura about him. If he said something, people tended to listen..." And on all teams he played the same role. A Green Beret instructor remembered:

"Scott was the sparkplug that every team needs."

Jaynie notes: "He was rambunctious, but always kind. His father observed that he never said a cross word to his sister, Connell, whom he viewed with pride and love even when they were very young."

Jackie Swaidan, a high school classmate, recalls him holding the door for her and greeting her when they had classes together. There are pictures of young children, the son and daughter of a fellow soldier, clutching fast to Scott's legs.

And he was always patriotic. As a small child, he would "roam around singing 'Grand Old Flag.'" He would stand erect "in a solemn and sacred ritual" at the playing of the National Anthem. He loved stories of historical figures who put the nation's welfare above their own. As his friend Xander Berry wrote:

"For Scott, honor and service weren't mere platitudes, they were integral elements of his being."

He also put unbelievable effort into any task, had unbelievable physical stamina, a great attitude and a high threshold for pain. One time he returned home from an outing with 150 mosquito bites. He just "shrugged them off." He excelled at Outward Bound, and in another summer, Scott and his friend Denny Lowe spent three weeks on a Rustic Pathways trip to Thailand. Denny recounts:

"I remember Scott being the hardest worker at a remote construction site in the mountains of northern Thailand, covered in mud, carrying boulders uphill while the Lisu tribesmen stared, astonished that Scott was smiling."

A fellow Green Beret concludes:

"Scott was by far the hardest working, most ambitious young soldier I have ever met."

As Scott entered his senior year in high school, he faced a dilemma. He had been recognized at a National Merit Scholarship student, was being recruited for football, and had unlimited personal, collegiate and career options. But in his heart of hearts, he wanted to be a soldier. Not necessarily an officer, and certainly nobody in a staff or support position. He wanted combat. But everyone else in his class was definitely going to college. His father was an esteemed economics professor, his mother a multi-degreed executive. Yet Scott's passion was to go straight to the military.

This decision was not a simple one for Scott. He was genuinely curious intellectually, and loved learning, but wondered if he could craft together his own education on his own terms. His "band of brothers" from the football team were all heading to college, and he had the opportunity to play at the next level. Mostly, I think, he wished to honor his parents, and his father had devoted his life to liberal arts and education at Occidental College. He decided to enroll at Pitzer College in the fall, liking the Claremont model of multiple schools in close, cooperative proximity, the diversity, and the football program. But he regarded it as an experiment rather than a commitment.

He had a fine freshman football season at Pomona-Pitzer, and Roger Caron, who heads the program, remembers Scott as "one of the toughest and smartest players I've ever coached." He did fine in his classes, but by December he wondered if he should take his final exams. Reminded by his father of the difference between a withdrawal and a flunk-out, he completed his work commendably. But in January he sat down with his parents. He did not want to return for his spring semester.

"I could drink a lot of beer, I could have a lot of fun, but I want to move on to something that feels like it matters more."

He would join the military as soon as possible.

Scott always wanted an opportunity to join Special Forces, but as someone without formal military training, it would be hard to find that pathway immediately. Over the December holidays he took a military aptitude test—physical and intellectual—without telling anyone. He also didn't mention for a while that he earned a rare perfect score, never being one to brag about his grades. Once it became clear that the Marines were non-committal in their offer to him, he turned to the Army, where he discovered an enlistment option called 18X, a pathway giving inexperienced candidates with promise the opportunity to try out for Special Forces. Scott would face eleven steps in an effort to become a Green Beret, as the second youngest in the class, in a program with a historical 10% pass rate. Of course he was excited, rather than intimidated, and on the day he signed he beamed happily: "Mom, I'm going to be a soldier."

The steps included basic training, advanced infantry and airborne, and proficiency in another language. Scott chose Arabic. He took a six month comprehensive course with three exams, the final one being a half-hour conversation with a native speaker. He passed. He passed everything, and became one of only three in his platoon of thirty-eight to become a Green Beret.

That level of success was only the beginning. He became qualified as a sniper, finishing in the top two of his class, which is why pictures of him in Afghanistan show him carrying two rifles, "a pretty heavy load," his mom says, "for a guy his size." He also wished to be assigned to a combat dive team. Only 5% of the Green Berets become combat divers, so he took an arduous seven week course in Key West, a challenge that reminded him of his ninth grade cross country run up Old Mammoth Road.

When he wasn't undergoing training at a special site, his home was Fort Campbell, Kentucky, with a storied group that had been commissioned by President Kennedy when he established the Green Berets. Scott had his own apartment, and entered a new "band of brothers" to add to his community of high school football friends.

"Scott kept grounded in both worlds," Jaynie, remarked. He lived among his tight group of soldiers, but kept close contact with family and friends. On phone calls he'd be full of questions: How was Connell's soccer going? Had they met X's new girlfriend? Was the story about Y losing his wallet true?

After three years, when given the opportunity to leave the service or stay, Scott had only one question: Would he be deployed overseas? Confident that he would, he re-upped.

His first deployment in 2013 was to Lebanon for six months, a training trip on which he worked with Lebanon's version of Navy Seals, in cooperation with our own Navy

Seals. Scott loved interacting with the Lebanese people, and there is a priceless video of him dancing among Lebanese soldiers, eventually placed upon their shoulders, the star of the show. A few minutes later we see Scott talking to them seriously, very much the man in command. Lebanon was not a combat assignment, although the group was near the Syrian border, poised for action. The next assignment would be different.

Scott spent the remainder of 2013 at Fort Campbell, and made it home for the holidays and for his fifth year high school reunion. At that time, he spoke to his parents about his future, a bit, but noted that "I think of my life in three year increments." He knew that next month he would be heading for Afghanistan.

When he began his combat mission he knew it would be multi-dimensional, not only fighting and training, but also interacting with local villagers, whom they would try to keep safe. As an NCO sergeant, Scott had command responsibilities, and was often required to plan his own missions. One day the top sergeant in the U.S. Army spoke privately to Scott, saying, "You guys are doing the heavy lifting."

True to form in his bi-weekly phone calls home, Scott

was full of questions, but talked little about his missions, knowing that phone security was easily breached. On June 5, toward the end of his scheduled deployment, he wished his mother happy birthday.

Jaynie said, "You're over the line, Scott. I understand your missions are done."

There was quiet on the other end. "You have wrong information, mom."

Several days later, Scott's team was assigned to assure that a village in southern Afghanistan was safe to conduct elections without interference from the Taliban. Their job was to clear them out so the election could proceed. They were out for thirty-six hours, less than an hour from their final pick up on June 9, chatting about what they would eat when they got back. Scott favored a chicken enchilada.

Two minutes later the Taliban fighters appeared. Scott immediately started running toward the action. SSG Brendon Branch says:

"When Scott charged up that hill to return Taliban fire it cost him his life, but it probably saved mine.
I'll never forget him."

On July 10, 2014, Army Staff Sergeant Scott Studenmund was buried at Arlington National Cemetery. A horse-drawn caisson carried the flag-draped casket to its place of rest. In the distance, a lone bugler played Taps. A soldier gently folded the flag, went to one knee, and presented it to Scott's mother, Jaynie. Extended family, friends, and both "bands of brothers" were present. I stood next to one of the toughest and turned away when I saw the tears on his cheek.

"Scott brought out the best in people and both inspired and challenged me to become who I am today," wrote friend Daisy Ross.

Said classmate and teammate Peter Denton: "Whether Scott knew it or not, everybody loved him. One reason for this was that he never acted like he was better than anyone else, even though he was better at almost everything."

George Washington once wrote:

*"Few men have virtue to withstand the highest bidder."*

During his twenty-five years, Scott Studenmund paired his private passions to the virtue of sacrifice for the greater good. This virtuous patriot ran up Old Mammoth Road, up

Fair Oaks Avenue, and finally, up the hill in the moment of truth, secure in his passions, secure in his values, the most confident advancer of all.

## DENNIS LOWE '08:
*The Virtuous Citizen*

I have called Scott Studenmund a virtuous patriot, who proved that he was willing not only to pledge "life, fortune, and sacred honor," but fulfilled his pledge on the battlefield, putting his country and the lives of his comrades ahead of his own. Scott was a true soldier, who spoke of a possible long-term commitment to the military. He had found a home.

One of Scott's dearest friends from high school, Dennis Lowe, is also a soldier, who entered United States Military Academy at West Point following his graduation from Flintridge Prep. Currently, he is serving as a platoon leader in Kuwait. He is proud to serve his country for his current five year term of duty, but may wish to explore other options outside the military. Dennis has a lot of interests.

The first clues to multiple passions came in kindergarten, when Denny decided that he would start a museum in the family home. He would begin with rocks, and cleared out his closet to make room for his expanding collection of specimens. I'm not sure where he put his clothes. Annually throughout childhood he would visit the Tucson Gem and

Mineral Show, a renowned international gathering of hobbyists and professionals. Eventually the museum expanded into various artworks and artifacts, requiring a larger commitment to space in the Lowe household.

Dennis came to his interests naturally. His father had begun collecting in his twenties; he and his cousins, and eventually his sister, were artists. Dennis was also an enthusiastic student at Flintridge Prep, where he appreciated "a staff dedicated to academic excellence. I was stretched by the rich environment to examine the world and my place in it. I was particularly lucky in my history classes." His favorites were Advanced Placement U.S. History and Mike Mullins' History of Warfare.

The military was another early interest. "I wore army costumes at Halloween, would talk to my dad about his time in the service, and began to collect items of military history."

Another interest was football and the band of brothers spirit that it fostered, as well as the discipline that it required. "Scott and I shared both football and the military. By the beginning of my senior year, I was dead set on securing an appointment to the Academy."

Dennis had worked extremely hard in his studies, particularly in math, which did not seem to come particularly easily to him, but which would be vital for future engineering classes. In the fall he received a "letter of assurance" that he would be admitted if he could secure a nomination from his representative or senator. He spent months working with all the official offices, and eventually was supported by Congressman Adam Schiff. He was in.

His next challenge was to get in the best possible physical shape for the brutal summer basic training, and Scott was there to help him.

"We had a friend named J.C. who was a marine, who helped us train hard, smoking us in every workout to give me a sense of what I would face. Scott was with me every step. I saw how he threw himself into every workout. The next year, when he told me he was going to try for Special Forces, I said, "Yup, that's what you need to do, Scott.""

Soon after his high school graduation, Dennis reported to West Point.

"They call it Reception Day. You say goodbye to your parents and then spend the summer with Cadet Basic Training, known as "Beast Barracks." During Beast, new cadets learn the fundamental soldier skills and begin their four-year process of leader development. Some come in with a skewed perspective of what it's going to be and drop out the first day of the first summer. West Point will find your weakness and help you address it. If you don't address it, you'll fail."

Dennis was not used to being yelled at, and found that West Point has little tolerance for mistakes made more than once. Throughout the first year, he worked out, cleaned barracks, and did laundry for upperclassmen—essentially experiencing the life of a private. The Academy made sure that each cadet experienced the military at all levels. Yet these extra responsibilities were secondary to academics.

"Like at Prep, I took courses across the curriculum, from philosophy, psychology, history, and art history, to math and science. I majored in political science, with an emphasis on global studies. Everybody takes math and engineering, which worried me because I didn't think I was good at math. But West Point doesn't give you the option to say 'I'm no good at math.' You learn it or get kicked out!"

Like he had done at Prep, he sought out extra help in any subject that challenged him, and also become a computer programmer. "I am by no means a programmer. The important thing was gaining the confidence to teach myself subjects that I would have previously avoided." Like Carol Dwek of Stanford advises, he overcame the "fixed mindset" of obsessing on native ability, and adopted the "growth mindset" of working hard and expecting to learn.

"You realize your mind is much more flexible than you imagined. I gained confidence in areas where I was not comfortable. I learned a lot about myself and the person I wanted to be."

Each summer, cadets conduct military field training and have the opportunity to attend training schools at other active duty installations. One summer he chose air assault, learning how to rappel and safely sling-load cargo for rapid transport anywhere on the battlefield. The premium is on precision, since any mistake can cost lives. During the summer before his junior year he served as cadre for Beast. This time he was the one responsible for instilling discipline and training a group of brand new cadets. It is hard to imagine one with Dennis's mild personality screaming orders.

"I had to put on a mask to yell and be extremely strict to shock soldiers and break down resistance. The trick is to learn when to flip that switch or not. That summer I probably learned as much if not more than the new cadets about leadership. Looking back on that experience, I realize I still had a long road of growth ahead of me and still do. I did see good leadership examples and bad ones."

During his final year Dennis made plans for his next five years in the military, the term of duty he owed his country for his education.

"Class rank is determined by three factors: academics (most heavily weighted), and physical and military attributes. Your rank determines the choices you will have upon graduation." Denny got assigned Fort Carson, Colorado, but first got leave to travel in Europe, then spent six months in Armor Basic Officer Leaders Course—a mixture of classroom instruction and field training—at Fort Benning, Georgia. A commissioned lieutenant, he arrived at Fort Carson in early 2013, with a key goal of becoming a platoon leader immediately.

"I did not get a platoon initially, but was assigned as adjutant for the Battalion Commander. I was upset at first, but was given an opportunity to sit in on meetings on strategy at Fort Carson and eventually in Kuwait, where I met with Kuwaiti officers. I was a fly on the wall for some amazing conversations. For me it came down to what attitude I was going to take into this situation, and I ended up learning things other platoon leaders didn't."

He received his platoon in the fall of 2013 in Kuwait, overseeing sixteen soldiers in tanks, a combination of veterans and rookies. They returned to Fort Carson in 2014, but were once again deployed to Kuwait in early 2015, undermanned, with only three soldiers in four person tanks. But they were prepared to move to Iraq, Syria, or Jordan if necessary.

"There's a ton of chaos over there right now. A lot of people play both sides. If ISIS comes to your neighborhood, you capitulate or lose. Part of our mission is to provide the regional U.S. commander with a robust response option if the need arises."

Denny is on a nine-month deployment, prepared, if necessary, to battle a force whose vision is a total conquest of all former Muslim land, including Spain. He has summoned the habits and perspectives of his broad background to be ready for anything.

Dennis, however, has his own vision of a life beyond the military, as he transfers his values of public service from the Army to civilian life.

"There are a lot of significant problems in the world, and we all need to step up. We have so much capacity and knowledge at our disposal, the Library of Alexandria at our fingertips on Kindle. The other day a soldier told me matter-of-factly that he's never read a book. He's self-selecting out of a world of knowledge. That's a big problem if you extrapolate over American society as a whole. People choose leaders, and we need good, ethical people running things."

Dennis believes in Robert Hutchins' conviction that a purpose of education is to prepare members of a democracy for citizenship, not merely by voting, but by assuming general stewardship of the republic.

"We have a responsibility to give back where we have the opportunity. In *Man's Search for Meaning*, when Viktor Frankl describes times in a Nazi concentration camp, he says there are decent and indecent men in every society. The battle between the two will determine if the decent people will achieve the lion's share of the influence to guarantee a flourishing society."

The first priority for Dennis: a serious national commitment to public schools.

"We had a fantastic education at Prep. I appreciate it more all the time. But there's got to be a way to give more people similar chances."

At eighteen, Dennis wrote: "As you go on your journey, internalize the wisdom you learn, then you will no longer need the books. Live the teachings rather than just read about them."

Lieutenant Dennis Lowe takes up the mantle of public virtue from his beloved comrade Scott Studenmund presently as a soldier in the Middle East. He plans eventually to come back home to Los Angeles in hopes of advancing education, the arts, and political responsibility to reignite the true American Dream in all its ethical and civic glory.

# COMMON **THREADS**

Across those sixteen profiles—three mentor/models, two contemporaries and eleven alumni, common threads link their stories together. As we watch all of them advance confidently in the direction of their dreams, we observe similar traits, attitudes and experiences that propelled them on their journeys. While sixteen examples is a modest sampling, they represent multiple fields: medicine, law, business, non-profits, science, the arts and global engagement. They offer evidence of the broad array of options and the multiple pathways open to young people in this century. As Robert Parker '78 once remarked, "It's not where you go to college, but how you go to college." And, I might add, it's how you pursue life before and after college. These sixteen stories, spread over almost a century, reveal seven common qualities that brought success, happiness and admiration:

## 1.   THEY PURSUED THEIR PASSIONS.

First and foremost, each of the sixteen refused to settle for a life that fell significantly below their dreams. While they were realists who constantly re-calculated their GPS according to circumstances, and often modified the specific logistics of their quest, they remained steadfast in insisting upon lives and careers that were engaging and inspirational. All sought true vocations. Some, like Tom, Chris, and Bryan, found their passion early while in high school. Others like Carrie, Naomi, and Rachel, tried many different things, and took the time in college and their twenties to experiment in a variety of fields, seeking the common denominators they found rewarding. But all remained hopeful and confident, eschewing fear-based decision-making for aspirational choices.

## 2.   THEY EXHIBITED STRONG DETERMINATION.

Each expressed resilience, grit, emotional stamina, and effort. Each of them faced challenges, some of them overpowering, but nobody submitted to defeat. I've watched Jordan Spieth play golf throughout last year, fashioning one of the

most remarkable seasons in golf history at age twenty-one.
I've noticed that whenever he makes a bogey or even a double bogey, he usually birdies the next hole. Spieth accepts
a setback, gets over it quickly, and digs in. Contemporary
parents and educators are sometimes accused of withholding
the gift of failure from children, and the charge may have
merit. Do we rush in to protect, with high grades, prizes and
perpetual do-overs? When I meet with students during their
senior year and beyond I'm reminded how much they value
a setback in retrospect, and how often they identify their
favorite classes as their most challenging.

Each of our sixteen subjects faced challenges—some of
them physical, such as Scott and Dennis in military training, some circumstantial, such as Vas's, Chris's and Megan's
disappointments on their graduate school paths. But all had
the resilience to fight back against pain and disappointment,
work extraordinarily hard, and have confidence that their
efforts would pay off. And they were right.

**3. ALL WERE LIFELONG LEARNERS.**

Robert Hutchins proposed "interminable liberal education." Each of the sixteen learned how to learn, and sometimes taught themselves as they faced unanticipated prob-

lems that no narrow training could prepare them to solve. All were intellectually curious, genuinely enjoying using their minds, drawing from a broad-based educational background. Almost all had the benefit of an education that helped them to think comprehensively and creatively across disciplines. Tom's English and environmental studies, Megan's literature and science, Deborah's English and medicine, Carrie's business and psychology, Bryan's art and history, Denny's political science and engineering, and Vas's science and policy studies all combined multiple fields. And all were readers. These examples support Fareed Zakaria's contention:

> *"A broad general education helps foster critical thinking and creativity. Exposure to a variety of fields produces synergy and cross-fertilization."*

Time after time, these sixteen faced circumstances requiring these intellectual qualities. And they were up to the task.

**4. ALL EMBRACED ENTREPRENEURIAL QUALITIES.**

In his article "Five Characteristics of Entrepreneurial Spirit" Matt Ehrlichman identifies five qualities our profiles share to an uncanny degree:

1.   "In tune with their passion"

2.   "Always question how it can be done better"

3.   "Optimistic about all possibilities"

4.   "Take calculated risks"

5.   "Above all, they execute"

All of those profiled have managed their lives and
careers as if they were startups, stemming from a personal
fascination. Each is a life in dynamism: Tom heading for
law school, Carrie's, Chris's and Vas's graduate work, Bryan
and Denny imagining lives beyond the Middle East, Megan's
next book, Naomi's three developing projects. They chase
improvement out of a hopeful spirit, confident in the future
and their own abilities. One can't craft a quality life out of
fear-based decisions, and each of our profiles learned not
to eliminate, but contain, fear, and refuse to be paralyzed
by uncertainty. That optimism led them to take calculated
risk, such as Carrie's jump from Deloitte to Gates, Deborah's
decision to have two children during residency, and Bryan's
photography in the Middle East. And finally, all acted on
their dreams, assuming full responsibility for their actions,

avoiding the victimization that blames somebody else for one's setbacks. As Vas realized at twenty, his decisions in college created his challenges for medical school admission, and it was up to him to overcome them.

**5. ALL FOUND MENTORS OR ADVISORS.**

One can go through life figuring everything out for one-self, but it's easier to find help. While each of these profiles had a strong independent streak, they benefitted from the wisdom and perspective of more experienced people, and often sought them out. Academic advisors helped Debo-rah, Megan, Vas and Mark Salzman imagine entirely new opportunities. Naomi's Nicaragua projects are inconceivable without the encouragement and alliance of Spanish teacher Manuel Nuñez. Carrie and Rachel have sought out veterans in the workplace who recognized their strengths and helped accent them. Having people who know deeply the campus-es, workplaces, and larger environments where you seek success, and who know you, can bring perspectives hard to find anywhere else. An advisor might be someone you meet once, but the encounter could be life transforming. Vas woke out of his confusion after hearing tough talk from a faculty member, and propelled himself toward medical school.

A mentorship might be a long-term relationship with a teacher or friend who understands you well enough to help with your self-awareness as you make crucial decisions. Parents can often serve this function. Without exception, each of the profiles spoke of the crucial support they received from parents at pivotal moments. In these cases, the adage that we get fired as parents, but, if we're trusted, get hired back as consultants, proved particularly true.

**6.   ALL HAD TRANSFORMATIONAL EXPERIENCES OUTSIDE THE CLASSROOM.**

As I conducted interviews with the profiles, I kept waiting for the moment when they would mention internships or opportunities abroad, and I was never disappointed. Time and again, people cited summer internships as windows into their future, informing and inspiring them. Tom knew he would be an environmentalist after his summer in Wyoming. Chris's summers in Germany ignited his passion for aerospace. Megan loved her work on a newspaper, and is now an editor. Naomi and Carrie both received job offers from Deloitte following their experiences.

Similarly, most benefitted from time abroad, immersed in other cultures, becoming as Carrie put it, "the other," and learning to navigate unfamiliar languages, customs, political and economic systems. Bryan's semester in Jordan was his pathway to a decade in the Middle East. Nicaragua utterly shaped Naomi's vision for her future. Rachel's multiple-continent living experiences clearly affected her global perspective, while Vas received classical medical training in England. Megan's year in a Nicaraguan fishing village led to her appreciation for scarcity and the environment. Each returned with an increased understanding of the world's complexity.

**7. EACH PURSUED A LARGER PURPOSE BEYOND THEMSELVES.**

In his 2015 book *The Road to Character*, David Brooks questions the emphasis on personal passion, fearing that this method "starts with the self and ends with the self." These profiles may start with the self, but that insistence on personal fulfillment led them to larger goals, more closely resembling the question posed by novelist Frederick Buechner:

> *"At what points do my talents and deep gladness meet the world's deep need?"*

Bryan believed the world needed to know the truth about war in the Middle East, and as a photojournalist sought to capture it. Megan thought we ate badly and threatened the planet, and wrote to awaken us. Deborah and Vas wished to heal. Carrie, Rachel and Naomi imagined a creative interplay among profit and non-profit organization to improve global health, relations, and opportunities. Scott and Dennis served their country in the military.

Each of these people refutes the fear that pursuing dreams is self-involved and narcissistic. To a person, they emerged from their quests devoted to public purpose, all imagining the world a better place. They saw, rather than a conflict, a cohesion between personal soulfulness and the greater good.

# EPILOGUE:
## *Freedom*

One additional thread running among these sixteen people profiled is the zest with which they used their freedom. With confidence they imagined and created options original to them.

In 2010, forty years after our first class together, Stephen Greenblatt published *Shakespeare's Freedom*. His opening line sets the standard:

> *"Shakespeare as a writer is the embodiment of human freedom."*

Yet Greenblatt is quick to note that Shakespeare's historical circumstances were anything but free, although he was.

*"Though he lived his life as the bound subject of a monarch in a strictly hierarchical society that policed expression in speech and print, he possessed what Hamlet calls a free soul."*

Robert Hutchins' teaching partner Mortimer Adler distinguishes between circumstantial and spiritual freedom, quoting a concentration camp prisoner: "I am not responsible for my circumstances, but I am responsible for what I make of my circumstances." By thinking and writing in the horrific conditions of the camp, Adler argues, the prisoner retained spiritual freedom the entire time. Greenblatt explores the degree to which Shakespeare as the artist is challenging the dominant values of his age while remaining a subject in a highly restrictive society. A bound subject with a free soul.

And a highly successful subject, to be sure. Shakespeare's plays were huge commercial hits, allowing him to invest in significant real estate and retire to Stratford before he was fifty. His plays were presented to aristocrats and two monarchs. He was a canny realist, who in his work, according to Greenblatt, "establishes and explores the boundaries that hedge around the claims of the absolute." Absolute authority. Absolute beauty.

In the chapter "Shakespeare Beauty Marks," Greenblatt explores the degree that Shakespeare, with his portrayal of many women, challenges conventional notions of beauty. Creating cultural context that draws from architecture, painting, and poetry, Greenblatt establishes the Renaissance "cult of featureless perfection." The times upheld absolute standards of body image, and celebrated the conventional dream girl. Yet many of the most interesting and alluring Shakespearean heroines fly in the face of convention: dark skin instead of light, birthmarks, moles on breasts. As Greenblatt observes, "Individuation shatters the ideal of featurelessness." The women feel free to assert their confident individuality, just as Shakespeare feels free as an artist to create these women. He feels free to be Shakespeare.

Several years ago, Stephen sent me a copy of *Shakespeare's Freedom*. By that time he had published another book, *Swerve: How the World Became Modern*, which would win the National Book Award and the Pulitzer Prize. It was of course widely heralded but controversial; Stephen had never shied away from controversy, steadfast in

his search for meaning among obscure and often neglect-
ed cultural artifacts.

A month after receiving the book from Stephen, I was
given a second copy by my son Rob as a Christmas present.
I was struck by the coincidence, until I realized it was no
coincidence, since my son valued both Shakespeare and
freedom. He had studied Shakespeare over a summer in
Oxford, and was Bach's grandson. Upon graduation from
college, with my role model's blood coursing through his
veins, he took off for Washington, D.C. with no job prospects, confident he would land something. Before he left, a
close family friend told him he was crazy. Yet his devotion
to dreams led to a year on the presidential campaign trail,
a position on the presidential transition team, a congressio-
nal committee assignment exploring the financial collapse,
graduate school at Columbia University, and opportunities
in social entrepreneurship. On May 23, 2013—Bach's 100th
birthday—I watched Rob receive his master's degree.

On that Christmas day I sat with two copies of the same
book, one given to me by its author, my twentieth century
teacher, the other by my millennial son—two threads of my

life who have never met, knitted together by a sixteenth century poet, his vision inspirational to each of them.

---

Often I take a bike ride along the coast in Ventura to see a friend. Technically she's an inanimate friend—she's a statue. But she's full of life and she's been admired for over four hundred years.

At the end of Souther Point, where one looks left to the harbor and right to the beach, she's focused on the center straight out to sea. If you sit with her a while, you see boats coming calmly through the gentle harbor, some of them choosing to remain in the protected spaces. Others, however, head straight for the ocean, undeterred by the rougher waves, knowing their boats will steady in time.

When you approach the statue, you see that she's the mermaid that Oberon recalls to Puck in Shakespeare's *A Midsummer Night's Dream*. He tells of her effect on the elements. A plaque on the statue carries his description:

*"Once I sat upon a promontory,*

*And heard a mermaid on a dolphin's back*

*Uttering such dulcet and harmonious breath*

*That the rude sea grew civil at her song*

*And certain stars shot madly from their spheres*

*To hear the sea-maid's music."*

The mermaid on the point is beckoning us from the harbor and the beach, pointing straight out to sea, with all its beauty, its roughness, and its potential.

The mermaid and her poet seem confident, urging us forward, promising nothing, but suggesting possibilities. Possibilities open to us when we are free.

# APPENDIX

Anyone tempted to consider those profiled in this book as outliers should note the comments of Flintridge Prep graduates. What follows is a representation of the confident dreaming that hundreds of our high school seniors have expressed when describing their version of the "good life" in their final Great Books papers. Organized alphabetically, these students reflect, in one sentence, the ambitions of hundreds more.

**Melody Aaron** '07: If someone simply tries to emulate the good life of another, he or she will probably find it does not fit.

**Agustin Acosta-Ghioldi** '14: Don't be a slave to others' ideas.

**Tom Adams** '06: The world is our playground, our canvas for artwork.

**Chris Adams-Cohen** '10: There are too many stories of dissatisfaction, of settling, and of discontent.

**Shannon Adelman** '09: Holding oneself with confidence and assurance can change a lot about how a person feels about himself, giving him the drive to pursue the good life.

**Suzy Allcroft** '03: The only way I will achieve the good life is if I am living a life that is uniquely of my own creation.

**Michael Areinoff** '99: I don't desire luxury, but rather the old surfer's inner peace.

**Charley Ayres** '12: I want to give service to society and those I care about.

**Anna Badalian** '08: Self-awareness is the key to choice. We must be aware enough to make our own choices towards the life we wish to lead.

**Abhi Banskota** '02: In my good life people are free to choose work they truly enjoy, rather than work jobs they hate solely to further other needs.

**Arielle Baptiste** '12: Don't sell ourselves short.

**Caitlin Barry** '06: The synthesis of other people's ideas has made one that is uniquely my own.

**Ben Bascom** '04: One cannot allow what one knows in their heart of hearts to go unsaid.

**Andrew Beck** '06: Man is meant to soar, so why not strive for excellence?

**Kate Beck** '09: The good life is the examined life  a consistent effort to find the best way to live.

**Shaira Bhanji** '10: The good life consists of knowing yourself, following your passions and seeking the best with the resources you have been given.

**Lisa Bierman** '03: A recipe for a good life should make people's individuality shine throughout, not oppress it.

**Cody Boyce** '08: Though the textures of the storm in the background of my song suggest turbulence, the melodies resolve themselves on a major chord.

**Katrina Boyd** '12: The past helps us with choices for the future.

**James Bradley** '12: Make choices in the deepest part of our souls.

**Carla Carpenter** '00: It is good to dream, and it is healthy to hope.

**Celene Carrara** '08: I am incapable of living quietly or desperately. The good life develops as we imagine and configure it.

**Sammy Case** '15: It's just the choice...It's the freedom of thought, of being able to control your own destiny.

**David Chen** '01: Happiness is finding your place in the world, who you are, and accepting it.

**Peter Chesney** '04: Passions are what make a good life, for they provide a reason for life.

**John Chi** '99: I couldn't listen to anything but my heart.

**Brian Choi** '01: By knowing your time is limited you realize it is precious.

**Melody Chu** '08: I take from Thoreau a zest for living.

**Julia Clark** '14: Avoid the sea of conformity.

**Rob Cobb** '96: I must hope and dream to have a good life in which I can have the freedom to live in harmony with others.

**Alex Conforti** '07: Please allow me to live by my own standards.

**Crystal Cook** '02: Individuality is part of what makes life interesting.

**Elizabeth Cook** '01: When I discover my passion, I hope that I will have the courage to fulfill it.

**Anne Costner** '02: Moments that turn our lives into art.

**Gina Crissman** '11: Freedom is a means to the good life, but what one does with freedom constitutes the end.

**Tizoc Cruz-Gonzalez** '00: A person needs to believe they can live the good life before they have a chance of living it.

**Luke Currim** '11: My good life is the drive for a fresh experience.

**Max Davison** '05: The moral of this story and the moral of this song is that one should never be where one does not belong.

**Jeff Defond** '10: People should become more self-aware and listen to what really fulfills them.

**Alicia Dewell** '11: Passion is the spice of life.

**Linda Donaldson** '08: The good life should constantly be breaking down façades.

**Sharon Donaldson** '06: The good life will always benefit from a healthy sense of wonder.

**Christina Dorobek** '04: In the end it is still up to you; you have to make the most of your good life.

**Diana Dou** '06: Mediocrity is the same as selling out…the good life means owning the horizon.

**Paul Dragna** '12: The key is confidence.

**Alexander Dugas** '96: We will only be truly free once we learn to think and live for ourselves and for the truth.

**Hannah Edwards** '09: When you look back at your life, no matter how your bank balance reads, it will be your actions and the injustices you fought or silently tolerated that define who you are.

**Kyle Edwards** '08: Mainly, I want to live without regret. I don't want to wake up years down the road and think, 'if only.'

**Lugene El-Harazi** '11: To live the good life, you need to be confident with yourself. Know your strengths. Know your weaknesses. And know how to be comfortable with both.

**Kyle Eschen** '11: We cannot live our lives as static human beings, lest we become a cell-chiseling alcohol off a liver wall.

**Jennifer Fairbanks** '04: Contentment is realizing there will be times when you will have to stand alone and being OK when your convictions are more important than what people think.

**Charlie Fellows** '15: The good life is a place safe for the individual to think and flourish on his own independence.

**Dyllan Fernandez** '10: The good life lies in the choices you make and the paths you take to get a credo that works well for you.

**Kevin Flynn** '10: The beauty of life is the beauty of infinite malleability, infinite possibility…when it appeals to the better angels of our nature.

**Simone Fried** '06: You have to take into consideration what sparks true joy into the depths of your soul.

**Lisa Friedman** '05: I must have the courage to find my own good life and the courage to live in it.

**Eric Fung** '14: Do not be conformed . . . You can start a renewal of your mind.

**Evangel Fung** '03: It is time that I became Martin Luther King's thermostat and fight the way the world thinks, instead of letting the world change me.

**Caroline Furman** '04: I hold creative and profound thought as essential to the good life.

**Olivia Gaines** '13: I have responsibility for my own dreams.

**Henry Gammill** '08: The good life can be boiled down to one word: choice. I alone wield the power to determine my own fate.

**Harper Gernet-Girard** '04: The value that I believe should precede all others is independent thought.

**Christoph Geiseler** '00: My good life is having the freedom to act, think, and believe in whatever I want…don't stop me and I won't stop you.

**Jessica Gerard** '10: Not using your mind power or your will is just letting the purpose of life go to waste.

**Lauren Gerard** '13: Why would I want to lose sight of my passions?

**Reza Gheissari** '10: Free will must be cultivated by allowing people to choose the path they take and choose their own good lives.

**Billy Goldstein** '05: The flight of the human spirit. Seems to me that's the only thing worth bothering about.

**Michael Graff** '09: You have the power to make your own good life no matter what anybody says.

**Matthew Grobar** '10: The good life is out there for people who refuse to quit, seeking it.

**Lauren Guarino** '11: The good life is living in the perpetual crispness of the dawn.

**Hunter Haney** '05: You must pursue your passions to be happy…if you think you don't have this chance, than let's have a chat.

**Briana Hedman** '01: It's hard to live by what you really believe in. It's much easier to say than actually do.

**Jennifer Heil** '02: I have the tools to make fateful decisions.

**Kristin Heintz** '07: The plan is to live life on my own terms and take complete ownership of my destiny.

**Lauren Hekman** '15: Try as hard as you can to empty your minds of the thoughts that say, 'I want this because it will make me look good.'

**Emani Holyfield** '11: As Fr. Robert Lawton says, 'embrace the adventure of becoming deeply and fully ourselves.'

**Audrey Horwitz** '10: The good life is a conscious effort…It needs to be thought out and worked at.

**Seth Horwitz** '03: Never let yourself be sucked into something you do not want to do, because when you look back, you do not want to regret monumental decisions you made.

**Lindsey Hunt** '15: It's okay to take time to think things through, and it's okay to be really really confused sometimes.

**Alex Jacobs** '07: Without taking risks, humans get lulled into a sense of complacency and utter mundanity popularly known as normality.

**Alex Jacobs** '08: Balance is the key to the good life. When longing balances satisfaction, a certain harmony exists.

**Lauren Jacobs** '14: Give me…independence of mind.

**Cari Jeffries** '10: As Lucille Ball says, 'It's a helluva start, being able to recognize what makes you happy.'

**Nolan Jimbo** '11: A life devoid of passion and emotion cannot bring man to his ultimate end--happiness.

**Chelsea Johnson** '14: I seek a life filled with what I hold dear.

**Kerstin Johnson** '96: The good life is a life in which each person has the freedom to find his own beliefs and to follow them. The best way to lead life is to always be true to yourself.

**Matt Johnson** '03: I believe we should take advantage of every opportunity given to us because it may not come again.

**Natalie Karbelnig** '08: I want to feel all filled up. By the rain. By desire. By passion.

**Lydia Kay** '09: It is important to have figures that we can look up to.

**Kristen Keen** '99: I would never give up anything that is special to me.

**Charlie Kennedy** '10: Undying curiosity . . . to continuously refresh our minds with new thoughts, experiences, and ideas.

**Kate Kersting** '13: Work toward your goal and lose yourself in the moments along the way.

**Alina Khodadian** '09: I remember asking my dad when he started his own business and he said he didn't want anyone telling him how to spend his time.

**Sean Kilmer** '14: Boredom is the cardinal sin.

**Chae Kim** '15: Often times, society will enforce one road. However, following another's path is identical to give up one's identity.

**Ken Kim** '01: For me, there has to be some sort of meaning for life, so that I feel I'm not wasting my time.

**Shelly Kim** '11: Moments of beauty, inspiration, transcendence that remind you of who you are and what you value.

**Katie Kimble** '03: The good life is allowing oneself to make choices wisely, without ignoring the sun beating down or the waves crashing.

**Claire Kinder** '08: The greatest type of wealth is curiosty, which constantly sets a new goal and awakens us with an infinite expectation of the dawn.

**Scott Kinder** '05: Making something out of nothing, I believe, is one of the fundamental needs of society.

**Sameer Kulkarni** '02: Each man must be capable of discovering his own sort of happiness.

**Christina LaBarge** '08: I need to be true to my self. I will appreciate the life I have been given and celebrate my individuality.

**Sebastian Langdell** '02: The choice is yours, and in the end, you will effect the change.

**Kate Laurents** '04: The good life is the free life, in which people have the opportunity to live according to their own natures and needs.

**Ben Lee** '96: I hope to find my own calling as Prospero did, by restoring and maintaining order, defeating my enemies and helping my friends.

**Victoria Lee** '01: In my art, the ocean serves as an open door to their potential as full human beings with intellect and emotions.

**Michael Leslie** '13: Stand up for what you believe in.

**Ryan Leslie** '11: People have become so concerned with looking outward that they pass over the answer everywhere they look.

**Larry Leung** '99: Indulge in your good life fantasy and it will become real in your mind.

**Audrey Levy** '14: No complacent homogeneity.

**Grace Lilienthal** '06: Acquire an ability to transcend custom and common conditions to craft intellectual originality.

**Diana Lim** '00: I will go where my heart finds itself at home...the wholesome, soulful joy in partaking of life.

**Jessica Linden Swienckowski** '04: To be true to yourself--to follow your mind, heart, and soul....this is living the good life.

**Kaitlin Liston** '14: Live life to the fullest.

**Judy Liu** '00: I want to put my heart into expanding other people's perspectives.

**Erin Loadvine** '09: Never underestimate the power of a little elbow grease and hard work.

**Sami Lubega** '01: I don't want to base my identity on other people's perceptions. I don't want to sacrifice my character to fit into a new environment.

**Kate Lyon** '12: I need to be true to myself.

**Rachael Madore** '05: Sometimes it can be simple to follow the majority, but at the same time the easy way can be dangerous.

**Jordy Manker** '11: Too often people look back on parts of their lives and regret things they have not done.

**Marcy Manker** '06: The good life is about constant growth and education…the various shapes of my puzzle pieces are only starting to emerge.

**Jill Marucut** '10: My good life asks me to create my own passions, not to discover it.

**Olivia Markowitz** '15: It is important to decide your own individual moral standards without society's imprint dictating your beliefs.

**Jessica Marter-Kenyon** '03: Sometimes we must act on our instincts and our gut beliefs.

**Jerome Martin** '97: Living the good life is a rebellion of sorts…we have to grab hold of life and hug it to our chests…seek the fabulous.

**Connor McCann** '10: If each of your actions has a positive effect on the next, the actions and their results begin to compound.

**Mary McCluggage** '07: It is necessary to find a passion and never let it go.

**Matt McCluggage** '05: One could never be truly happy if one never met or recognized their full potential.

**Daniel McLaughlin** '08: The good life can be attained when we have the moral courage to act as well as we possibly can.

**Jack McLaughlin** '10: My good life is like my fingerprint, specific only to me.

**Jackson McHenry** '11: The good life is ultimately the free one.

**Sonora Miller** '10: I want to be able to tell my great-grandchildren that I did all that I could, tell them stories that will inspire them to live their own good lives.

**Evan Monroe** '15: I want to cross my bridge without a compass.

**Ben Naecker** '05: My good life will not wait for me. I must be the one to begin it. I must be the one to take control of my own life.

**Jeff Naecker** '04: Not what to think, but how. Learn how to ask the right questions and find out what is true for yourself.

**Rachel Nagrecha** '02: I want to share the gifts which stem from my soul with the world.

**Zack Newman** '03: I might as well shoot for the top.

**Andy O'Connor** '96: Prospero's excellence has gained him his freedom.

**Laura O'Connor** '00: Living is up to you. Nobody can dictate to you what your definition of living is.

**Daniel O'Leary** '10: Time is our most valuable asset, we cannot buy more of it or slow it down; we can only appreciate it.

**Raquel Olvera** '11: I want to have the courage, the passion, the wisdom gained through the experience of a complete life.

**Ansley Orona** '06: As Thoreau says, 'If a man does not keep pace with his companions, perhaps it is because he hears a different drummer. Let him step to the music he hears, however measured or far away.'

**Taryn Orona** '09: If we must march to a different beat, then let us all be out of formation in exaltation.

**Chris Osborn** '97: Spend your time on whatever makes life worth living.

**Jen Ouyang** '06: Having people I can always return to gives me the confidence to branch out.

**Olivia Ouyang** '10: I think that the choices between which desires are more important are the decisions that define us.

**Heather Owen** '99: Life cannot be good where you are a stranger to yourself.

**Adam Paiz** '01: I have to analyze my life correctly. I do not want to miss the deep signs or hidden clues that affect my happiness.

**Janice Park** '10: As flawed as humans appear to be, they are inherently rational and moral and should they choose to pursue it, have the capability to achieve the good life.

**Lexy Parnass** '05: People are only "sterling" in character until they have reached self-actualization and become independent, realistic, and non-conformist.

**Emily Parry** '99: I believe the struggles we encounter on a daily basis add to the good life, not detract from it.

**Laura Perry** '05: It is a man's character that determines his worth, not his wallet or religion.

**Sarah Peterson** '05: Everything I know and learn means little to me if I do not make some effort to share it with the world.

**Lori Pridjian** '14: The individual is the ultimate decision-maker.

**Nitya Rajeshuni** '09: While it is important to understand the reality of our dreams, we cannot be intimidated by the possibility of failure.

**Sarah Randolph** '10: I keep my dreams big, for how else can I demonstrate the power of my life.

**Brian Reardon** '04: When one is engaged, he is living life as it should be lived.

**Katie Reardon** '99: Embrace the tension between growth and familiarity.

**John Rodli** '10: Freedom to pursue the good life independent of societal or state influence is the key.

**Brandt Rohde** '15: Rather than love, than money, than fame, give me stories. My life has always been, to me, a collection of narratives that weave in and out of one another, but all connected by their presence in my life.

**Kellan Rohde** '12: Be pragmatic and optimistic.

**Marissa Roy** '10: In my good life, intellect is a huge priority. True intellect is originality of thought.

**David Russell** '11: Live morally, selflessly and faithfully to the cause of making the world a better place.

**Lexy Ryan** '08: A little self-confidence never hurts.

**Jasper Ryden** '12: Sincerity.

**Katharine Schwab** '11: In my good life, give me the ability to wonder.

**John Seaver** '98: One cannot be fullfilled if he believes one way on the inside, but chooses not to pursue those feelings through outward action.

**Nick Seaver** '03: The good life is our sole responsibility and for our lives to have any meaning we must find our conviction and pursue it.

**MacLean Sellars** '99: I live by my own path. The minute my theory on the good life no longer holds true, I will rip it down and find a newer, better and more complete one.

**Jenny Seto** '05: Pursue those dreams and use them to become happy and prosperous.

**Mike Simon** '05: My goal is to take the road less traveled, while enjoying the journey of life each and every day.

**Lenea Sims** '11: Dream up a beautiful future.

**Jasleen Singh** '09: Some can spend their lives trying out different jobs and hobbies looking for their function, but it's much more beneficial to look inward first.

**Marina Smith** '05: We must all sculpt our own lives if we are to feel any satisfaction at their end...the clay may differ, but sculpt we must.

**Sarah Smock** '04: The good life is lived to be an example to the lives around it.

**Andrew Stein** '04: First and foremost, I will be self-confident. I will remain an individual as well as a contributing member of society.

**Leanne Stein** '01: I know better than anyone else what I need to be happy.

**Jon Stoeckly** '03: Loyalty and passion to beliefs and principles.

**Alec Storrie-Lombardi** '09: If your parents, school or friends were to choose who you were going to be, it would be like someone trying to make a puzzle piece fit where it's not supposed to be.

**Connell Studenmund** '12: Give me compassion...I hope to practice medicine because I like the science but primarily I want to give back.

**Jacqueline Swaidan** '08: Whether or not we feel ready to handle a lighted stick of dynamite, we must.

**Catherine Swaidan** '13: I need to be honest with myself.

**Tony Tartaglio** '04: I fear that it may be a while until we see another American revolutionary idea put forward.

**Gianna Taylor** '07: Normal people worry me.

**Ben Teitelbaum** '04: I will not stop the search for who I am.

**Sophie Teitelbaum** '07: As my grandpa always said, 'Life is about being rich in the important things.'

**Katy Thompson** '05: The best part of the good life is that it changes.

**Kylie Thompson** '08: The passion that accompanies one's actions is the strongest indicator of a lasting good life.

**Denise van der Goot** '11: Freedom is necessary--your own freedom to make decisions and follow your passions.

**James Vandeventer** '09: Each great writer evaluated ideas with an immense air of content self-confidence.

**Hannah Vaughan** '05: As Borges wrote, 'If I could live my life again, I would..take more risks…make more trips…I would have more real problems and less imaginary ones.'

**Anton Verbinski** '14: A person has to shape and build his own good life.

**Pooja Verma** '05: She took the pieces of life that fit her hopes, and became a part of them.

**Sam Wald** '99: I'm living the good life as long as I have a purpose and the free will to pursue it.

**Shelby Wax** '12: We should strive to improve the world.

**Chloe Wayne** '06: I will never reach my full potential if I am not prepared to walk through rocky paths to get there.

**Doug Weber** '97: Not propriety…wakefulness.

**Lauren Weinberger** '07: To me, the good life involves experimenting to find a passion, taking a risk for something I love.

**Michael Weinstein** '14: Pursue your passion and interest . . . wisely.

**Natalie Weinstein** '10: The good life is what you make of it.

**Isabella Weiss** '11: Each person is an individual and therefore has their own version of a good life.

**Raymond Weitekamp** '06: I think there can be no greater goal in the good life than a complete understanding of oneself.

**Brandon Wen** '11: The good life comes from the freedom obtained in fighting for one's own morals and living by personal beliefs.

**Cameron Wen** '15: I do not want to be accepted by others by conforming to them.

**Elliot Witter** '15: When people ask me what my dream job is, I reply that it is to be Renaissance man.

**Ashley Suarez Wood** '08: The good life is freedom. Once freedom is achieved, you can focus on a balance between your material and emotional needs.

**Monica Woodward** '06: I find one aspect of the good life a sense of optimism. Optimism is free.

**James Woolley** '07: I know one thing for sure, and that is if one can satisfy his soul, he will be living the good life.

**Dylan Yamamoto** '09: Abraham Lincoln says, 'Most folks are as happy as they make up their minds to be.'

**Kate Yandell** '06: You reserve judgment for the moment when you will know it is time to make an important choice and you hope in that moment you will have the rare experience of absolute clarity.

**Andreana Yasuda** '04: One must root out what is false to perceive what is true.

**Sandra Yum** '00: I don't know what my passion is, but when I find it, I hope it will drive my life.

**Chris Zaro** '15: ...To put myself in a place where I can continue to grow, making my melody louder and my harmony more pronounced.

**Allan Zhang** '10: The good life is entirely self-determined.

**Madison Zeller** '09: We want not only a good dream, but also a good life when we wake up.

# ACKNOWLEDGEMENTS

First and foremost my thanks to the twelve subjects who spent extensive time with me telling their stories, and to Jaynie and Woody Studenmund, who shared memories of Scott. I was constantly inspired by these conversations, as I was by the hundreds of Great Books students in The Appendix and beyond who are advancing confidently.

Many people generously offered valuable feedback on the text along the way: Molly Bachmann, Rob Bachmann, Sarah Cooper, Judi Kalitzki, Kim Kinder, Mark Kriss, Rachael Madore, Mark Salzman, Robert Skotheim, Nicole Trevor, Paul Vandeventer, and Madison Zeller. From start to finish, Claire Kinder was my steadfast partner with administrative and editorial support.

My memories of time with Bach Bachmann, Robert Hutchins, and Stephen Greenblatt fuel each day of my life and work.

To quote my son Rob:

"Gratitude may be the supreme value since so much proceeds from it."

La Cañada, 2016

## A NOTE ABOUT THE AUTHOR

Peter Bachmann received his A.B. in History from the University of California, Berkeley. He received his M.A. in History from the University of Virginia. Since 1980, he has been a faculty member at Flintridge Preparatory School in La Cañada, California. Since 1991, he has served as Headmaster. He lives in La Cañada with his wife, Molly.

CPSIA information can be obtained
at www.ICGtesting.com
Printed in the USA
FSOW03n0726210616
21782FS